HORSE RACING'S
STRANGEST®
TALES

Other titles in the STRANGEST series

Titles coming soon

HORSE RACING'S STRANGEST TALES

Extraordinary but true stories
from over 200 years of racing

ANDREW WARD

PORTICO

First published in the United Kingdom in 2017 by
Portico
1 Gower Street
London
WC1E 6HD

An imprint of Pavilion Books Company Ltd

ISBN 978-1-911042-46-4

A CIP catalogue record for this book is available from the British Library.

10 9 8 7 6 5 4 3 2 1

Reproduction by Mission Productions Ltd, Hong Kong
Printed and bound by Bookwell, Finland

This book can be ordered direct from the publisher at www.pavilionbooks.com

CONTENTS

INTRODUCTION

Horse racing is delightful bait for strange events. In 1935, for instance, a murder trial in the Bahamas was abandoned for the day at lunchtime – so that court officials, jury and lawyers could attend a Montagu Park race meeting. Jury members were given a police guard. If anyone enquired, they were presumably told that the jury was out.

These strange tales are mostly set on conventional racecourses but, as horses have fared well against a variety of non-equine competition – men, dogs, motor vehicles, Olympic swimmers and Olympic athletes – the book includes some offbeat examples. I've concentrated mainly on British horse racing, with a few stories from elsewhere in the world.

The starting-point for the book – the early 19th century – is arbitrary and to the detriment of some earlier strange races. In 1377, Richard II, then Prince of Wales, lost a match to the Earl of Arundel. If Richard III would have given his kingdom for a horse, no doubt Richard II would have traded his for a better one. Going back to the 18th century would have meant including races against time, such as Miss Pond's 1,000 miles (1,610km) in 1,000 successive hours at Newmarket in 1758, but not Lord March's amazing racecourse bet that he could have a letter carried 100 miles (161km) in an hour. This wouldn't qualify because Lord March didn't use horses, relying instead on 20 cricketers with safe hands to throw a ball (containing the letter) in a big circle for an hour. He won his bet.

Strange races have themes – weather, stray dogs, great victories, depressing defeats, odd locations, tragic circumstances, etc. – but the strangest are those unimaginable ones that sneak up on horse racing fans. They include the riderless horse that won a race, a 3,200-mile (5,150km) horse race won by a man on a mule, and a victorious deceased jockey. In 1923 Frank Hayes posthumously rode *Sweet Kiss* to victory at Belmont Park, Long Island, after suffering a fatal heart attack on the run-in. His body stayed in the seat until the winning-post and then fell to the floor.

In the modern era strange races continue to emerge. Horses have competed against dogs, humans, stock cars and bicycles, while pantomime horses now have their own race. In the 1990s there were two peculiar Grand Nationals, and a 2010 race saw *My Wife Knows Everything* and *The Wife Doesn't Know* finish first and second.

WOMAN AGAINST MAN
YORK, AUGUST 1805

At the age of 22, she rode side-saddle against the best male jockey of her generation. She was dressed for the race, wearing a purple cap and waistcoat, nankeen-coloured skirts, purple satin shoes and embroidered stockings. Fit and healthy, she was a fine jockey, a spirited woman, and the race was a thriller.

The 2-mile match between Alicia Meynell, riding Colonel Thornton's *Louisa*, and Frank Buckle on Mr Bromford's *Allegro* was watched by a huge crowd on York's Knavesmire racecourse. The previous year Alicia Meynell (also known as 'Mrs Thornton' though there is some debate as to whether she was really married) had ridden a horse called something like *Vingarillo* – there are various spellings on record – in a 4-mile match against Captain Flint's *Thornville* but had been forced to ease up her lame horse after leading for the first 3 miles. Captain Flint spent the next year claiming he was still owed 1,000 guineas of the 1,500 guineas prize. Colonel Thornton, in response, argued that the extra 1,000 guineas was nominal – to attract people to the racecourse.

Alicia Meynell, daughter of a Norwich watchmaker, had moved to the Thornton estate near Knaresborough, where she was 'under the protection' of Colonel Thornton. Both she and her man had an eye for a fair racing match, and the contest between *Louisa* and *Allegro* caught the public's attention. The spectators on the Knavesmire that afternoon would speak of the race for years to come.

The match took place at 3.30 in the afternoon, and Alicia Thornton took *Louisa* to the front. The ace jockey Frank Buckle – his career record of 27 wins in English classics was unsurpassed until Lester Piggott – rode a waiting race, as was his usual style. Having bided his time, Buckle brought *Allegro* to the fore, ready for the run-in. But the side-saddled *Louisa* fought back, and the two horses raced neck and neck for the winning-post. The race was won by *Louisa* by a short neck. A victory for the woman.

Wrote *The Times*: 'The manner of Mrs Thornton's riding is certainly of the first description; indeed her close seat and perfect management of her horse; her bold and steady jockeyship, amazed one of the most crowded courses we have for a long time witnessed.'

It seems a shame to spoil such a heroic victory by the realities of the race, but I must mention the weights. Mrs Thornton carried 9st 6lb (59.9kg), Buckle 13st 6lb (85.3kg). The difference of 4st (25.4kg) might have affected the outcome of a race won by a short neck.

The other harsh reality of the afternoon was the appearance of Captain Flint at the racetrack. Still believing he was owed money from the previous year's match, Captain Flint brought out a new horse-whip and began flailing it at the shoulders of Colonel Thornton. In the presence of ladies, it was not the done thing. The crowd hissed and hooted at Flint, and the Lord Mayor ordered his arrest, leaving Alicia and Thomas Thornton to count their winnings in peace.

OUTSIDERS FOR THE ST LEGER

DONCASTER, SEPTEMBER 1822

'What? Ride a cripple like that!' John Jackson is supposed to have exclaimed when he was told he was riding *Theodore* in the St Leger. When he learned that a bet of 100 guineas to a walking-stick had been laid on the horse winning the classic, Jackson was not uplifted.

The jockey was distraught and tearful when told that the horse's owner was exercising his right to call on him to ride *Theodore*. It was a ride Jackson would rather have missed. The horse might have been passable as a two-year-old, but as a three-year-old was showing pathetic form and was rumoured to be lame.

The general odds on the horse were around 100 guineas to one (some were offering 200–1) and the 'walking-stick' bet, an outlay of something worth about a shilling, showed up the horse's chances. According to some expert opinion, the horse might need the walking-stick to get round the course.

'We are positive that the annals of sporting history never produced an occurrence on which such anxious doubt existed as on this race,' wrote *The Times*.

The 3–1 favourite *Swap* was nowhere, while 'Mr Petre's *Theodore* took it into his head to run quite contrary to the opinions of owner, trainer, jockey, and everybody else who entertained an opinion on the matter.' Jackson got the horse off well at the start, and kept him going. The spectators were excited but amazed when they saw three complete outsiders pass the winning-post first. *Theodore* won at 100–1, while second and third both came in at 50–1. 'The most favourite horses were either distanced or lost.'

Perhaps never in horse racing history have three horses of such long odds come home in a major race, and rarely has a walking-stick been so well invested. And, as another strange feature of this race, the four horses trained by James Croft finished first, second, third and fourth. The following day, *Swap*, the unplaced St Leger favourite, beat *Theodore* at level weights to provide another curious result.

THE COCKED-HAT STAKES

GOODWOOD, AUGUST 1824

The cocked hat, a three-cornered hat with a permanently upturned brim, was fashionable at around the turn of the 18th century. Hence the expression 'to knock into a cocked hat', meaning to alter something so that it is unrecognisable.

The cocked hat was a gentleman's hat, and, in the early 1800s, races called Cocked Hat Stakes were popular with gentlemen. They took two forms. In one every jockey in the race was compelled to wear a cocked hat when riding. In the other cocked hats were optional, but a weight advantage (6–7lb/2.7–3.2kg)) was granted to those who complied with the appropriate dress.

A Cocked Hat Stakes was run at Doncaster in 1820 – 'the unusual head-dress of the jockeys caused much curiosity and much merriment at the scales' – and at other venues, including Hampton, Goodwood, Shrewsbury and Oswestry. At Hampton, in July 1823, Mr Braithwaite appeared at the scales in a hat only 'half cock' and there was much discussion about whether he should claim the 6lb allowance. A writer in the *Sporting Magazine*, quoted by John Fairfax-Blakeborough in *Northern Turf History* (Vol. 3, p. 269), thought cocked-hat races rather too cockeyed: 'Gentlemen jockeys, generally speaking, look enough like jockeys when dressed in proper caps and jackets; but when they adopt the costume of a dancing master to ride a race, they cannot but appear highly ridiculous and quite out of character. I need not say I refer to cocked-hat stakes. I am not going to applaud Mr Braithwaite for the altercation it seems he occasioned at Hampton, by not having the regulation "cock", because if he had not approved of the articles he need not have entered his horse.'

As an example of a bizarre Cocked Hat Stakes, here is one from Goodwood, where such races continued until around 1829. On Friday 20 August 1824, a Goodwood race was 'ridden by Gentlemen in Cocked Hats'. The five horses included Lord George Bentinck's *Olive*, who had already raced once that afternoon. But when *Olive* dead-heated with *Swindon*, the two horses were forced to run-off over the same course of three-quarters of a mile, the gentlemen wearing the same cocked hats. *Olive* and *Swindon* dead-heated again, so they tried for a third time. This time *Olive* came through to win.

'This was an admirable race,' commented Pierce Egan's *Life in London*, which may simply mean that the riders, wearing cocked hats, looked more like admirals than jockeys.

A RACE
AGAINST THE CLOCK
NEWMARKET, NOVEMBER 1831

Squire George Osbaldeston was considered by his contemporaries to be 'the best sportsman of any age or country' according to Theodore Cook, editor of *The Field*, who wrote the introduction to the Squire's belated autobiography, published 60 years after the great sportsman's death.

Squire Osbaldeston (1786–1866) turned his hand to all sports, and bet on steeplechasing, hunting, trotting, cricket, rowing, royal tennis, billiards, shooting and whist. He once won a bet playing royal tennis with a gloved hand (and a few points' start) against a champion who held a racket, and his friends would wager on outrageous feats such as covering 100 yards (91m) in fewer than 30 hops and eating 20 fried eggs within five minutes. Had there been a *Guinness Book of Records* in the 19th century, one suspects that Squire George Osbaldeston would have been a likely consultant editor.

Osbaldeston made a particularly celebrated wager in 1831. Taking his lead from a certain Mr Ridsdale, who claimed he could ride from London to York in ten hours, Osbaldeston offered to ride 200 miles (322km) in ten hours for a wager of 1,000 guineas. His challenge was taken up by General Charritie, and rules were drafted. Osbaldeston would ride over a 4-mile course at Newmarket – the Round Course and Devil's Dyke to the stand – on the Saturday of the

Houghton meeting. To win his bet he must cover the course 50 times within ten hours on as many hacks, hunters or other horses as he pleased. No time would be deducted for mounting, remounting, eating or dealing with any mishaps that might arise.

An ex-prize fighter called John Gully, then a renowned racehorse owner, was offered 10–1 against Osbaldeston completing the 200 miles inside nine hours. When he sought advice, the Squire indicated that he could achieve that time with a few better-class horses. Gully lent him some good racehorses and took the 10–1 offer.

At this time of his life, Osbaldeston was a 45-year-old sporting veteran with a permanent limp, a result of a compound leg fracture in a hunting accident ten years previously, his horse having been knocked over by another when about to take a fence. Wisely recognising that this event needed training, he worked up to 80 miles (129km) a day on the horses he intended to ride. Although his weight was not in his favour – together with bridle and saddle it was 11st 3lb (71.2kg) – he decided not to lose weight.

His famous wager of 200 miles against time started at 7.12 on the Saturday morning, attended by a big crowd. He covered the first 4-mile (6.4km) heat in nine minutes, a good enough pace if he could keep it up and move quickly between horses. But problems were always likely – one stirrup leather was a few inches longer than the other on one interchange and he decided on a meal stop after 120 miles (193km). That was a delay of eight minutes.

Changing horse every 4 miles, he pressed on and made good time, covering the first 100 miles (161km) in four hours, 19 minutes and 40 seconds. The biggest setback came when *Ikey Solomon*, owned by Mr Nash, threw him on to the ground and bolted on the 31st lap. Anticipating this possibility, the Squire had stationed men around the course to retrieve a bolting horse. *Ikey Solomon* was caught and remounted, but that 4-mile leg took 12 minutes.

With the Houghton meeting taking place simultaneously spectators were able to watch both events – the Squire continued to move from one horse to another. He rode John Gully's *Tranby* four times, and the horse rewarded him with a time of eight minutes for one 4-mile lap (the 27th).

Finally, having ridden 29 different horses, Osbaldeston completed his 200 miles. The time, including mounting, dismounting and refreshments, was eight hours, 42 minutes. He had won his wager and Gully had won his. According to one account, the Squire was none the worse for his arduous journey: 'There was no wrapping in blankets; no carrying to a post-chaise; no salts, smelling bottles or lancets. The Squire jumped on his favourite hack, *Cannon Ball*, and, followed by every horseman on the ground, led them at a slapping pace to his lodgings, at Perrin's, in Newmarket, where he got into a warm bath, took a nap, and in a couple of hours was wide awake and enjoying himself at a good dinner.'

As thanks to the people who had lent him horses, Osbaldeston offered a £50 Handicap Plate 'for horses that galloped in the match against time'. The race, called the Osbaldeston Plate, was won by *Timekeeper*.

A FAVOURITE FAILS ON THE FLAT

DONCASTER, SEPTEMBER 1835

They came no better than *Queen of Trumps*. She was an exceptional three-year-old, and 1835 belonged to her ... except for one strange race at Doncaster. Competing in the Scarborough Stakes, at incredible yet realistic odds of 1–10, she suffered one of horse racing's most unusual handicaps.

That year *Queen of Trumps* won the Oaks from *Preserve* with something to spare. Trained by John Scott, the filly came to the St Leger with a big reputation – 'she possesses great power and resolution, and is a free goer and of good temper' – and destroyed a strong field. *Mundig* and *Ascot*, first and second in the Derby, were beaten, and so too was *Preserve*, whose connections looked in vain for revenge for the Oaks defeat. As 11–8 favourite, *Queen of Trumps* proceeded gradually to the front of the St Leger field, accelerated when she needed to and 'won easily and cleverly, by a length and plenty to spare'.

When she headed a field of three for the Scarborough Stakes, three days after the St Leger success, *Queen of Trumps* had won six out of six for the year, including two classics. Despite carrying an extra 7lb (3.2kg), she was 1–10 favourite to take the race. There was hardly any betting on her two rivals, *Ainderby* and *The General*. Indeed, anyone betting against 'the Queen' deserved to be led in a strait-jacket into Lambeth's Bedlam.

They raced over a mile. *The General* took an early lead, *Ainderby* held second place, but Mr Mostyn's *Queen of Trumps*, the pride of North Wales, was simply biding her time, her strong, muscular quarters barely rippling. The three came into a line, and they reached the distance abreast.

At the merest of requests from jockey Tommy Lye, *Queen of Trumps* moved into the lead, ready to gain several lengths on her rivals in those last 100 yards (91.4m).

And then came the surprise. A big dog ran on to the course and darted directly towards the favourite.

Lye feared his horse would fall. He all but pulled up *Queen of Trumps*, who changed leg, swerved, and lost her place in the race. She was good enough to come back, but *Ainderby* held on to win by half a head – one of the greatest upsets in racing.

Captain Frank Taylor, owner of *Ainderby*, was apparently so confident of his horse's lack of chance that he was drinking in the bar while the race was being run. Someone ran in to tell him the story of how *Ainderby* had won in bizarre circumstances. Captain Taylor swiftly realised that his token bet, out of loyalty to the horse, would bring him £2,000. He searched the course for the owner of the big dog – one source says the dog was a mastiff, another that it was a bulldog, and a third that it was a 'big white dog' – and bought the animal. Captain Taylor kept the dog in luxury and eventually left it an annuity for life.

So the 1835 flat season ended with *Queen of Trumps* scoring six wins out of seven races, rather than seven out of seven. But she was not the same animal as a four-year-old. The reason for this may be the deterioration in form suffered by most four-year-old fillies, who, I am told, are notoriously difficult to train. Also, the heavy build of *Queen of Trumps* would not have helped her retain form … but I just wonder about the psychological effects of meeting a big dog at Doncaster when in sight of the winning-post!

This is far from the only example of horse meeting dog on a racecourse. Very occasionally the meeting was arranged. At Doncaster in December 1800 there was a curious match between a racehorse and a greyhound: 'A mare was started, and after she had gone a distance of about a mile, a greyhound bitch was let loose from the side of the course, and ran with her nearly head to head to the distance post, where 5 to 4 was laid on the greyhound. At the stand it was even betting, but the mare eventually won by little more than a head.'

The story does not explain how the greyhound was enticed to stick to the course, but John Fairfax-Blakeborough throws some light on how foxhounds were matched with racehorses on Redcar sands: 'Unfortunately the trail laid for the hounds was too strong and blew out to sea, so that the selected representatives chosen from the Cleveland Pack spread in all directions, and the race proved a fiasco.'

In general, though, racecourse meetings between dogs and horses were against the wish of stewards, and almost certainly against the wish of thoroughbred horses, who particularly dislike greyhounds. In fact it was common for the racecard to warn spectators that stray dogs would be shot. They could cause havoc, and, as will be revealed later (see page 164), have frequently done so.

VERY THICK FOG

CHELTENHAM, JULY 1841

Racing folklore is rich with tales of what really happens behind the walls of thick fog which commonly shroud racecourses. One concerns the jockey who hid behind a haystack and then reappeared ahead of the field on the second circuit to win easily. Another, a tale of morality, stars a jockey who tried the hiding tactic, reappeared several lengths clear on the second circuit and still finished last. And yet another story involves the jockey who took the hurdles so far on the outside that – by accident or design – he kept running round them in the fog.

There is, of course, a very dangerous side to riding in fog – as will be revealed later in the story of the race at Derby in 1889 (see page 60) – but it has to be admitted that fog produces a comic theatrical effect which entertains the imagination. Anyone who has watched a race on television and seen riders disappear into the foggy country must have wondered about what they could be up to. As recently as 1947, the connections of *Caughoo* had to face a lot of flak about what really happened in the fog – did he take a short cut? – after the Irish horse had won the Grand National by 20 lengths at 100–1. That occurred in a year when conditions were good for an outsider – a large field, bad weather which had disrupted training schedules and heavy going – and *Caughoo* had been well prepared on Portmarnock sands.

Cheltenham's County of Gloucester meeting of 1841 took place on the beautiful Cleeve Hill, which offered a splendid view of hills and dales, woods and fields, streams and rivers. Unless, of course, it was encased in very thick fog. Then you saw nothing. And Wednesday 21 July was one of those days. Moist, misty and miserable.

It was the second day of the meeting, and the opening race was the Sherborne Stakes, run over a mile. Recklessly, the officials pressed ahead with the race, and five runners went to the post, or went somewhere out of sight. Several other jockeys refused to ride.

The race, as it developed, was between the Duke of Richmond's *The Currier*, ridden by Sam Rogers, and Mr Griffiths's *Tupsley*, ridden by John Chapple. For all we know, the other three might have got lost in the fog or hid from their owners as the *Racing Calendar* informs us that they ran but were not placed.

Tupsley, romping home with a good lead, was ridden past the judge's winning-chair to win the race … or so Chapple thought. He didn't realise that what he thought was the winning-chair wasn't the winning-chair. He had pulled up too early. *The Currier* galloped past to win a victory for the Duke of Richmond … and the fog. Though how the judge expected to tell the two horses apart – both riders wore variations of yellow – is a mystery.

Now, the suspicious side of me wonders a little bit about what might have gone on in the fog. What do you think? Surely a losing jockey would be kind enough to point out to the winning jockey where he was on the course: 'Here's the winning-chair now, you've done it.' That's only etiquette, isn't it?

That one race was enough for the Wednesday's racing. It was agreed that the other races would be postponed until the following day. Any optimistic comments regarding the fog – 'It'll lift in a minute' – were obviously misplaced in this instance. After the Wednesday night dance, the good folk of Gloucestershire returned for the third and final day's racing, and the weather was good. *The Currier* and *Tupsley* were there again too. They raced on all three days, *The Currier* managing two firsts and a second, *Tupsley* scoring two seconds and a mistake which also counted as a second. By the end of the meeting, the two horses probably knew the course well enough to find their way round blindfold, or in a fog.

The best jest belongs to the *Cheltenham Examiner*, which went to press early on Wednesday 21 July, the day of the very thick fog: 'The early hour at which we go to press prevents our giving the returns of to-day's sport, which we expect will be first-rate.'

Yes, first-rate fog.

THE ADVENTURE OF RUNNING REIN

EPSOM, MAY 1844

The tale of the 1844 Derby is one of intrigue, mystery and roguery which could have come from the plot of a Conan Doyle story. Indeed Conan Doyle's *Adventure of Silver Blaze* contained some similarities. But in the case of *Running Rein*, the master detective was horse racing's own Lord George Bentinck rather than Sherlock Holmes.

In 1841, a foal was born to Mr Cobb of Malton. The bay colt, by *Gladiator* out of *Capsicum*, was called *Running Rein*. In November 1841, the animal was purchased by a Londoner called Goodman 'Goody' Levy, known as Mr Goodman around racing circles, where his reputation was shady. At almost the same time, Goodman Levy bought a yearling called *Maccabeus*. Both horses did the rounds of several stables.

In 1843 *Running Rein* won a race for two-year-olds and the identity of the horse was challenged. A stable boy, called in by the investigators, swore that he had been present at the birth of *Running Rein* two years previously. He identified the horse and the objections were dropped. The suspicions remained, with an extra one – that the stable boy had been bribed.

In 1844 *Running Rein* was entered in the Derby and looked a likely winner. By this time the horse had been sold to Mr Wood of Epsom and was trained by Smith at Newmarket. The stewards permitted the horse to start in the Derby, on condition that if he came in first the stakes would be withheld pending a further investigation into the horse's age. The same conditions applied to a horse called *Leander*, owned by the Lichtwald brothers, also suspected of being a four-year-old. The judge was told to note the names of the first five past the winning-post, just in case a couple were disqualified later.

The favourites for the race were *The Ugly Buck*, winner of the Two Thousand Guineas, at 5–2 and *Ratan* at 3–1, with *Running Rein* at 10–1 and *Leander* at 14–1. Twenty-nine went to the post, and the race had plenty of incident. Coming round Tattenham Corner, *Leander* had the lead from *Running Rein*, but the second horse struck *Leander*'s off hind leg above the fetlock. *Leander* pulled up lame, and an examination revealed a splintered bone. The horse was later put down.

The accident to *Leander* left *Running Rein* with a lead of 2 lengths, and jockey Mann kept his horse in front. *Running Rein* came home first by three parts of a length. Nat Flatman rode *Orlando* (20–1) into second place for Colonel Peel, and the Colonel also owned *Ionian*, which finished third at 15–1. Then the investigations began, much to the relief of one punter, Captain Osborn, who had put everything he owned on second-placed *Orlando* and was about to write a suicide note and blow out his brains when someone tipped him off that *Running Rein* might be an impostor.

Mr Wood, owner of *Running Rein*, fervently denied the claim that his horse was four years old, and defended his cause to the hilt when the case reached court on 1 July. The Lichtwald brothers did likewise on behalf of the deceased *Leander*, but examination of part of the horse's jaw showed the teeth of a four-year-old. The brothers, outraged by the accusation, dug up the remains of *Leander* and had his head cut off for further examination. The evidence again pointed to a four-year-old horse, and the Lichtwald brothers were warned off.

The *Running Rein* court case was more complicated as the owner didn't know where the horse was and therefore couldn't produce him for examination. (Someone claimed the horse was hidden at Finchley by Goodman Levy.) The outcome of the case, in which Mr Wood was the plaintiff and Colonel Peel the defendant, was sealed by Lord George Bentinck's cunning detection. Bentinck worked on the assumption that if a switch had been made by Goodman Levy, probably around September 1842 when both *Running Rein* and *Maccabeus* moved stables, it would have involved bringing the colouring of *Maccabeus* in line with that of the other bay colt. The four-year-old's legs had probably been dyed. Lord George therefore called on dye suppliers between Goodman Levy's home and club, and the move paid off at a hairdresser called Rossi in the Regent Street area. A woman remembered selling hair dye to a man answering the 'Goodman' description, her memory jogged by the fact that the man had ordered a second supply without paying for it. The dye was specially made, and Rossi himself had listened to the instructions. Lord George Bentinck took Rossi to see Goodman Levy and positive identification was made.

Goodman Levy had purchased hair dye at a time when he owned both *Maccabeus* and *Running Rein*. The most likely explanation was that *Maccabeus* had been dyed to resemble *Running Rein*. Moreover a Northamptonshire farmer called Worley had come forward to say that he had attended the Derby and the horse running that day looked a lot like *Maccabeus*, whom he had kept on his farm for a while. The evidence was conclusive. Wood withdrew from the case, *Orlando* was promoted to victory, Nat Flatman was supposedly given a present of £5,000 by Colonel Peel for the way he rode the winner, and Captain Osborn drew a sigh of relief as the new result spared him from bankruptcy and suicide. It was, however, a real slur on the integrity of horse racing as it cast doubt on some earlier Derby winners, especially the 1833 winner *Dangerous*, a 'three-year-old' who appeared only for the big race and was never seen afterwards.

At the end of the final case of *Wood vs Peel* before Baron Alderson and a special jury the judge observed: 'If gentlemen condescend to race with blackguards, they must condescend to expect to be cheated.' Goodman Levy and his associates fled the country, and *Running Rein* ended his days in peace on a Northamptonshire farm.

MAN AGAINST HORSE OVER HURDLES

LIVERPOOL, SEPTEMBER 1849

If you put the winner of the Grand National in a contest with an Olympic hurdling champion, who would you expect to win?

On pure statistics you would be a mug not to back the horse. The world-record 110 metres hurdles time shows that man can hurdle at around 19mph (30.6km/h), but this compares unfavourably with a top horse like *See You Then*, who ran the 1985 2-mile Champion Hurdle at about 30mph (48.3km/h), or *Red Rum*, who in his heyday managed the ferocious Grand National course at 30mph. Even a wind-assisted, steroid-assisted Ben Johnson would be stretched to improve on 23mph (37km/h) on the flat.

But what happens if you choose the best runner in the world and put him against an *average* horse? And what happens if you choose a short course of, say, 120 yards (110m), with eight hurdles close enough together to make the horse slow down?

Who would win – the horse or the man?

On a Wednesday afternoon in September 1849, a large crowd of spectators gathered in Liverpool at Mr Emery's ground at the corner of Great Homer Street and Kirkdale Road. They were considering just that question: who would win – horse or man?

The top runner of the day was a famous American called Seward, who was described as 'the champion of pedestrianism in England'. Seward bet £20 that he could run 120 yards and leap eight hurdles in a better time than a mare called *Black Bess*, then performing at the Queen's Theatre in Liverpool. Mr Harwood, the owner of *Black Bess*, would ride the horse over the 120-yard course. The wager was planned as the best of three heats.

Seward arrived at 4 o'clock wearing his white running kit. The mare, in stark contrast, was black and sleek. There was a great deal of betting, and the odds favoured the horse.

On a signal, they were off, and Seward took an early lead, soon to be caught by the horse. Seward and *Black Bess* raced neck and neck – or neck and shoulder if you prefer. At the seventh hurdle there was little between the two runners, but the ground sloped uphill at that point, favouring the horse rather than the man. Over the final hurdle, the horse edged in front, and *Black Bess* stormed through to win the first heat. The distance was recorded as 'a length', but it doesn't say whether it was a length of the horse or a length of the man.

After half-an-hour's rest they were ready to go again.

Seward again got an early lead and held it for most of the course. But when he reached the uphill part, he again fell back. There was little to choose between them at the last, but the mare got up in the run-in to win the second heat and the contest. The distance was half a length.

Almost 90 years later, in Chattanooga, Tennessee, a 120-yard hurdle race was organised between Forrest Towns, an American Olympic hurdle champion, and a prize cavalry horse called *Tommy Roberts*. Each jumped five hurdles set 20 yards (18.3m) apart, but the horse jumped high hurdles, the athlete low. Towns took an early lead and the horse toppled two hurdles before coming with a late run. The judge, left with a difficult decision, gave the verdict to the Olympic hurdle champion.

So now you don't know which way to bet.

THE WORST-EVER DAY'S RACING

KELSO, SEPTEMBER 1849

You may think you've attended some bad race meetings – some people may argue convincingly that there is no such thing – but not many can compare with the strange examples at Kelso in the late 1840s. In 1847 there were so few horses at the course that most of them ran at least twice. In 1848 there was one walk-over and one two-heat race of six horses. But the September meeting of 1849 had the most limited competition ever; only one horse ran ... and that walked the course. Not surprisingly, Kelso races were abandoned for a time, resuming in 1853.

The *Kelso Chronicle* did its best to make a news item out of the racing of 25 September 1849: 'The only stake to be run for at Kelso this year, was a Produce Stake entered into three years ago, when our race meetings formed the greatest attraction for sporting gentlemen in any place in Scotland. It was known previously that there would be a walk-over, and consequently the attendance of persons at the Race Course was very limited, and the whole did not occupy more than ten minutes.'

Perhaps the strangest feature of the meeting was that *anybody* would turn up to watch a day's racing that was limited to one walk-over. There's no accounting for taste.

The winner of the Produce Stake was Lord Eglinton's *Elthiron*, who, by all accounts, walked impressively over the course of 1½ miles.

THE LAST OF THE GREAT MATCHES

YORK, MAY 1851

The breathtaking events which led to the challenge match between the owners of *Voltigeur* and *The Flying Dutchman* in May 1851 occurred during the previous year's big races. First there was the Derby, then the St Leger and finally the Doncaster Cup, although it was only in the last of these that the two famous horses raced against each other.

The hero of 1850 was undoubtedly *Voltigeur*, Yorkshire bred, Yorkshire trained and owned by Lord Zetland. The Yorkshire public loved it when the horse romped home at 16–1 in the 1850 Derby, and they waited with high hopes when *Voltigeur* was pitched against seven comparatively ragged-looking beasts for the St Leger.

Yet the 1850 St Leger was itself a strange race. An Irish outsider called *Russborough* crept up and gave *Voltigeur* a neck-and-neck race for the line with the partisan Doncaster crowd willing *Voltigeur* to get there first. The judge ruled it a dead heat.

The spectators were even more involved in the run-off race, submerging the course from the Red House bend and leaving barely 4 yards' (3.7m) space for the horses to pass through. At the point where the crowd was at its densest *Voltigeur* looked beaten, but recovered brilliantly to snatch victory right on the line. Spectators waved handkerchiefs and threw hats in the air. The local hero had done it. He was now considered ready to race *The Flying Dutchman*, winner of the 1849 Derby and undisputedly the best horse around. Two days later the two horses met in the Doncaster Cup on *Voltigeur*'s home Yorkshire soil.

'It was a race between giants,' started an account by W. Greenwood, written in 1918. 'And never has there been such a "Coop Day" before or since. So strong a favourite was *The Dutchman* that the betting was 11 to 2 and 6 to 1 on him: but Marlow, who was not quite sober, made the pace so terrific from the start that, when Nat Flatman crept up on *Voltigeur*, there was nothing left to *The Dutchman* in response to the jockey's call; and the northern champion scored a thrilling victory by a neck.

'The crowd seemed to be quite paralysed and utterly unable to believe that such a giant as *The Dutchman* had fallen at last. His backers, we are told, wandered about pale and silent as marble statues; and Marlow stood near the weighing-room in a flood of tears, with Lord Eglinton, himself as pale as ashes, kindly trying to soothe him. As for the Yorkshiremen, they went mad with delight over their idol's victory.'

Lord Zetland and Lord Eglinton agreed to match their horses again the following spring on the Knavesmire at York. The distance was 2 miles. *The Flying Dutchman* carried 8st 8lb (54.4kg) and *Voltigeur* 8st (50.8kg), and the purse was 1,000 guineas a side, but what was really at stake was the reputation of the two horses. A witness described the match: 'When the flag fell *Voltigeur* went off with the running at the top of his pace, taking a lead of at least 3 lengths, and making very severe play, the heavy state of the ground being taken into account. In this way they rounded the last turn, when Marlow called on the *Dutchman* with a request very pointedly urged. As they passed the stand it was stride for stride, and a struggle of desperate effort. It was too much for the young one – he tired the sooner: and *The Flying Dutchman* passed the winning-chair first by a short length.'

It was called the 'race of the century' and was later referred to as the last of the great challenge matches.

THE UNITED KINGDOM TRAINERS' STAKES

LIVERPOOL, JULY 1854

Can you imagine a race where the horses are ridden by horse racing's top trainers rather than top jockeys? It happened for three years (1854–6) at the Liverpool July meeting, and the stakes were exceptionally unusual.

Racing Calendar described the division of the stakes and entry requirements as follows: 'The second recd. 10 sov. out of the stakes, and the last paid the stake of the third horse. The winner gave a dozen of champagne to the members of this race; ridden by professional trainers of five years' standing, who do not ride publicly or for pay in either flat races, steeple chases, or hurdle races; 1¼ mile (17 subscribers).'

The first running of the race, in 1854, brought five of the 17 budding trainer-riders to the starting-post. Robert I'Anson won the race and lost the champagne. His mount was the 6–4 favourite *Billy Richardson*. Messrs Owens, Taylor, Tempest and Wilson were the other riders, Mr Taylor riding his own horse, *Lady in Waiting*, into third place to claim his stake from Wilson.

The limited local publicity awarded to the Liverpool race meeting was overshadowed by that accorded an inquest into the death of a 15-year-old boy who was accidentally shot and killed while standing behind the boards at the back of a shooting gallery at the racecourse. 'Manslaughter by some persons unknown' was the verdict – several people were firing at the time – and horror was expressed at the limited safety arrangements at the gallery. The boards were a mere inch (2.5cm) thick, and a similar tragedy had occurred at Chester racecourse not long before.

The UK Trainers' Stakes survived two more years. There were four runners in 1855, when I'Anson won again, by 4 lengths on *Puritan*. Then in 1856 there was a problem. A field of only three runners meant that Mr Harrison, finishing third and last on *Meigh Dair*, won his stake from himself. Mr J. Watson won the 1856 race on *Prince Plausible*, three-quarters of a length separating second-place Robert I'Anson from a remarkable treble.

A QUADRUPLE
DEAD HEAT
NEWMARKET, OCTOBER 1855

'A most interesting and exciting race,' reported *The Times*. 'Up the cords they came side by side, and every inch of ground was so closely contested by *Gamester*, *Lady Golighty*, *The Unexpected*, and *Overreach*, that on reaching the chair the judge's decision was a dead heat with the four!'

Only a very unusual race warranted an exclamation mark in *The Times*, and the fifth race of the Houghton meeting, on 22 October, fulfilled all the necessary criteria. Only five horses were in the race, a sweepstake for two-year-old colts, and the fifth, *King of the Gypsies*, finished a mere half a length behind the four winners.

The original betting had favoured *Overreach*, who was 4–6, with the others all at 5–1. For the rerun, *Overreach* went out to 6–4, and the three other runners shortened to 3–1. It was another cliffhanger.

'A capital race was won by a head,' wrote *The Times*. 'Half a length between the second and third, and between third and fourth.' The winner was *Overreach*, with *The Unexpected*, *Gamester* and *Lady Golighty* following him to the line.

This quadruple dead heat came slightly more than four years after the one at The Hoo on 26 April 1851. At Gorhambury Park, near St Albans, the Omnibus or Open Hunters' Stakes ended with the judge being unable to separate Mr Land's *Defaulter*, Captain Broadley's *Squire of Malton*, Lord Strathmore's *Reindeer* and Mr Rayner's *Pulcherrima*.

Fusilier was beaten into fifth place by a head, and three others ran. In the rerun, *Defaulter* 'won cleverly by half a length'.

The only other quadruple dead heat in Britain was at Bogside on 7 June 1808. The first heat of a 2-mile race ended with four horses passing the post together. *Honest Harry* won the next two heats and took the race.

A UNIQUE FORMAT
SALISBURY, APRIL 1858

What a start to the race meeting at Salisbury. A unique format for the first race of the day. Unwittingly, the race was run by an elimination method.

Seven went to the post for the Craven Plate. The outcome was a triple dead heat between Lord Portsmouth's *Pinsticker* (6–1), Mr Blanton's *Polly Johnson* (5–1) and Sir J.B. Mill's *Bar One* (3–1). The 5–2 favourite, *Admiral of the White*, was unplaced. *Fugitive* was fourth past the winning-post, 2 lengths behind the even trio.

The three dead-heaters went back to the starter, Mr Hibburd, for a run-off. There was very little swing in the betting – *Bar One* was 7–4, *Polly Johnson* 9–4 and *Pinsticker* also 9–4 – and very little relaxation for the judge, Mr Manning. Although *Bar One* was a bad third, the other two horses again exercised the judge's eyesight. Another dead heat.

Mr Manning now had the field down to two. *Polly Johnson* and *Pinsticker* went to the post for the third time, and the betting was even. This race was also close, but *Pinsticker* got up to win by half a length.

This three-heat elimination race gave the meeting a good start. Even though the weather was cold and cheerless, the meeting was later considered to be Salisbury's best yet, and its new place in the racing calendar, between the meetings at Newmarket and Chester, was also claimed a success.

A RACE FOR STAYERS

CARMARTHEN, FEBRUARY 1862

In 'unpropitious' weather conditions of drizzling rain, over a severe 4-mile National Hunt course in the exposed setting of North Wales in February, *Ace of Hearts* and *The Rug* produced an amazing display of courage and stamina.

Races at Carmarthen, 4 miles (6.4km) out of the town, consisted of two laps of the 2-mile course. On Tuesday 4 February there were two such races. The first, beginning at 3p.m., was an open steeplechase which attracted six runners. *The Rug* set the early pace, then disputed the lead with *Gaslight* and *Ace of Hearts*. *Haphazard* fell, but the jockey remounted and made up the lost ground – 'several fields' – to get back in the race temporarily. *Pine Apple* fell, but the jockey wasn't fit enough to remount.

By the last fence, it was a race between *The Rug* and *Ace of Hearts*. The latter took the jump in the lead, but *The Rug* then came to the front. *Ace of Hearts* fought back and the two battlers reached the finishing-post together. The judge couldn't separate them. It was a dead heat.

Sir R. de Burgh, owner of *The Rug*, and Mr W.R.H. Powell, owner of *Ace of Hearts*, agreed to run-off the dead heat after the second race of the day. That meant the horses were subjected to another two laps of the 2-mile circuit, as was jockey Monahan on *The Rug*, although Mr J.R. James was injured in the second race and had to be substituted by George Stevens on *Ace of Hearts*. This was no disadvantage to Powell's horse. Stevens won five Grand Nationals between 1852 and 1871.

When the rerun started, at 5 o'clock, the light had already faded and *The Rug* was 4–5 to take the race. Halfway round the first circuit, *Ace of Hearts* fell while in the lead. The saddle turned right round and it took some time to adjust it. Stevens remounted and set off again, a hopelessly long way behind … except that *The Rug* was now repeatedly refusing at the fences.

The Rug still held a commanding lead at the end of the first circuit. Then he twice refused the first fence on the final circuit, almost as though protesting at having to go round again. *Ace of Hearts* was making ground all the time after Stevens' remounting, and the two horses took that fence together. They stayed together, all the way round the final circuit. They jumped the last fence together, galloped along the straight together and passed the finishing-post together. Another dead heat.

After 8 miles, the race was not yet decided. They would have gone round again, but night had fallen. The stakes were divided instead.

A few days later, the same two horses met twice in two days over 4 miles at Aberystwyth. *Ace of Hearts* won the first by a neck and the second by a more comfortable distance. In those days, horses certainly earned their feed, and those two needed to be good stayers.

A NEW RACE

SHREWSBURY, NOVEMBER 1862

Shrewsbury's new race, the Welter Handicap, of five sovereigns each, with 20 added, at first sight appears an insignificant event in the wealthy history of horse racing, but more detail of the race's background is revealed in the memoirs of bookmaker George Hodgman.

On the eve of the final day of Shrewsbury's autumn meeting, late in the racing season, four betting men bemoaned their serious plight. They were all broke. How could they recover some money?

Hodgman and George Angell arranged the new race and squared it with the Clerk of the Course. It was a small handicap, for gentlemen riders, with jockeys carrying 5lb (2.3kg) extra. Hodgman entered four horses – his own *Sheerness*, Mr Angell's *Astarte*, Mr Dunne's *Zora* and Mr Barber's *Abron*. He delayed public notice of the race until 4p.m. – the closing time for entries – but a fifth entry somehow sneaked in. This was *Tom Sayers*, owned by Mr Justice who raced as 'Mr Priestley'.

Hodgman sent for Angell.

'Here, George,' said Hodgman, 'there's a nice mess. Mr Priestley has entered *Tom Sayers*. What's to be done?'

'I don't know,' answered George Angell. 'But he's a wretched bad horse. Let him alone.'

'No,' said Hodgman. 'There might be an upset. We will go for him.'

'Good gracious. He's such a bad 'un. We can't.'

But they did. They arranged for George Fordham to ride *Tom Sayers*, a poor enough horse to attract good odds, and fixed up four trusted men on the other mounts.

Hodgman enlisted the help of George Payne and Ten Broeck. They put £1,000 on *Tom Sayers*, a horse consistently described as 'a brute'. The betting opened at 5–4 against *Sheerness*, and closed at evens on *Tom Sayers*, 4–1 against *Abron* and 10–1 against *Sheerness*.

When the five runners were sent away by the starter, *Tom Sayers* immediately showed his character by whipping round. Fortunately for the near-bankrupt punters, the other jockeys brought their horses back, even though it should have been a real start.

When they started a second time, George Fordham tried his utmost on *Tom Sayers*, while the other four jockeys knew what was required of them. *Tom Sayers* came home easily by three-quarters of a length.

The coup brought £2,500 for the £1,000 investment. It was split between four owners, four jockeys and one other. All benefited except the winning owner and Fordham, but the ace jockey roared with laughter when told the story. So that was why he hadn't been left well behind, as he felt he should have been.

But was it any wonder that Admiral Rous was beginning his campaign to stamp out some of the corruption on the turf?

AN EMPTY BOX
SALISBURY, MAY 1864

The quiet, cathedral town in Wiltshire was overflowing for the two-day race meeting, and accommodation was not easy to find. The first day at the racecourse was a long one, mainly because of false starts, and the next day, following the same pattern, was made even longer by an event which may be unique in racing.

It happened in the Stonehenge Plate, a race for two-year-olds over half a mile, the fifth of seven races on the second day, curiously Friday 13 May. There were four runners, two of them yet to receive names, and, when the race was run, one unnamed colt, a bay by *Vedette* and *Katie Stewart*, came through to win comfortably. *Dr Swishtail* was second, Mr Woolcott's brown filly third, and *Vera Cruz* fourth.

There were no objections, nothing for the stewards to be upset about: the start was good, the finish was clear, the correct course was taken and there was no reason to doubt the weights.

Yet the race had to be rerun.

Nothing untoward had happened except one thing. The judge was not in his box to see the finish.

Although most spectators could have placed the horses without dispute, the judge hadn't seen the finish, and the judge was the sole arbiter. So the horses went to the post again, the original betting still standing (except for bets placed between the first race and the rerun).

Fortunately, for all concerned, the four horses finished in exactly the same order in the second race. 'The colt by *Vedette*, out of *Katie Stewart*, twice won the Stonehenge Plate,' understated one newspaper.

So where was the judge when the colt won the first time? Had he sneaked off for his tea? Was he relieving himself behind a bush?

I wouldn't want to dwell on what the judge was doing out of his box – it had been a long day – but there is some evidence to suggest why he was caught out. To make up for lost time, in an attempt to finish the day's racing early enough for some spectators to catch trains back to London, the jockeys were ordered to the post for the Stonehenge Plate without cantering before the stand and then the race was started quickly.

The final word belongs to the *Racing Calendar*: 'This race was run twice with the same result. The first time the Judge was not in his box, and the stewards ordered the race to be run over again. For the first race the betting was 6 to 4 each against the winner and *Dr Swishtail*, and for the second, 5 to 1 on the winner. The actual race was won by 2 lengths, the same between second and third. The winner was sold to Mr W.W. Baker for 150 gs.'

A SAVAGE BRUTE
GOODWOOD, AUGUST 1866

The race for the Chesterfield Cup was the highlight of a Goodwood meeting that generally failed to reach expectations. Included in the field of 21 runners was *Broomielaw*, a horse renowned for his savage idiosyncrasies. Henry Custance was usually the unlucky jockey dealing with the brute. The Chesterfield Cup was no exception.

Broomielaw had won his first-ever race, the Dee Stakes at Chester, but gave early warning of his savagery by seizing hold of another horse halfway through the race and then kicking down the paddock railings afterwards. On the first day of the Goodwood meeting, Custance rode *Broomielaw* to victory in the Craven Stakes. That gave enough reminder that the Chesterfield Cup was to be no picnic ride.

Having been given permission not to canter to the start, Custance and the horse walked. As soon as the jockey hinted he was coming aboard the horse turned on him 'like a mad bull'. A coat was thrown over the horse's head to blindfold him and Custance was thrown on to *Broomielaw*'s back before he had a chance to think about it. The horse immediately displayed his temper by kicking, rearing and bucking, running Custance into the furze bushes and the countryside around Goodwood. 'We have had some experience of kickers,' wrote *The Times*, 'but, out of a circus, we never saw such an operator as Mr Chaplin's horse.'

Broomielaw's circus act went on for about 30 minutes with the other 20 horses waiting at the start. Custance was on his own to deal with the brute, as he later recorded in his autobiography: 'I tried all I could to get the assistant starter, who rejoiced in the name of "Squirt" Norton (he had lived with Mr Bloss as helper in the winter), to come and lead him back; but he knew *Broomielaw*'s little playful ways, such as biting off a man's thumb, so declined having anything to do with him.'

After the horse had had enough of kicking and rearing, he turned stubborn. Wouldn't move. Besides tearing the grass to pieces with his mouth.

'I can't wait for you any longer, Custance,' shouted the starter.

Custance pleaded for the starter to send over his man, and this was the last chance. 'Now hit him as hard as you possibly can below the hocks,' the jockey told the man, 'and then crack your whip.'

This sent *Broomielaw* off again, but, fortunately, in the direction of the start. The starter somehow got them away to a good start, and *Broomielaw* was in the leading pack, looking every bit as though he was going to bite off his rivals' heads. The savage brute won by three-quarters of a length at 100–8 and then entered the paddock on his hind legs.

The next week, setting off for Brighton, *Broomielaw* kicked his horsebox so hard that he was never the same horse again. His career ended after seven wins in 17 races … and a lot of incident.

ROBIN HOOD, ROBIN HOOD, RIDING FOR THE NAME …

NEWMARKET, OCTOBER 1866

In 1866, even the most informed connoisseurs of the track experienced some confusion. Two horses were running under the same name. One horse called *Robin Hood* was owned by Mr C. Alexander. The other horse called *Robin Hood* was owned by Baron Rothschild. Both were three-year-olds.

It couldn't happen today, of course, but it was not uncommon in the earlier days of racing. According to Reg Green, *two* horses called *Bedford* took part in the 1852 Grand National, one owned by Mr Chance, the other by Mr Elmore. Both fell.

The matter of two horses called *Robin Hood* really needed resolving, and the two owners did it in the most sporting way possible. They organised a race for the name, 'the loser to drop the "Hood"'.

The match took place towards the end of Newmarket's second October meeting – Mr Alexander's *Robin Hood* against Baron Rothschild's *Robin Hood*, the loser to be thereafter called *Robin*. It was one of the easiest races in history in which to guess the name of the winning horse.

I have traced no descriptions of the actual running, but I guess it went something like this: It's *Robin Hood* from *Robin Hood* … and now it's *Robin Hood* from *Robin Hood* … and the winner is *Robin Hood*, with *Robin Hood* in second place.

The entry in *Racing Calendar* was more precise: 'Mr Alexander's *Robin Hood*, by *Wild Dayrell*, recd. ft. from Baron Rothschild's *Robin* (late *Robin Hood* by *North Lincoln*), both three yr olds, 8st 10lb [55.3kg] each, D.M. 200, h. ft.'

After the two horses had raced for the name, Baron Rothschild's horse would no longer 'wear the hood', as *Sporting Life* so quaintly put it.

A STARTER'S NIGHTMARE

CROYDON, JUNE 1871

The meeting at Croydon, which took place on the first two days of June, provided enough problems for the starter, Mr Marcus Verrall, to give him nightmares for a long time. At 8 o'clock on the second evening, the jockeys still not under control for the final race, Mr Verrall had had enough. He threw down his starter's flag and returned to the weighing-room.

The signs were there on the first day. The first race started 'after much delay at the post', and the second race was a shambles: 'The competitors were on their legs when the flag fell, *Admiration* being at least 10 lengths in front, which advantage he maintained, and, making all the running, won by a neck.' The inevitable objection was sustained, the race was judged a 'flying start' and declared void, but *Admiration* still won the rerun.

For the fifth race on that first day, 'several of the jockeys were unruly at the post, and a long time was cut to waste, Prior being the principal offender'. As stewards now had the power to fine or suspend jockeys for misbehaving at the start – part of Admiral Rous's crackdown to improve racing – Prior was fined £5 for his sins, but worse was to come for the jockeys the following day.

The first race on the Friday ran smoothly, but the second had its problems for the starter: 'Upwards of an hour was cut to waste at the post.' Skelton and Payne were reported for 'disobedience at the post' and were later fined two sovereigns apiece.

The third race was run without mishap, but the fourth was slow to start: 'Another long delay occurred at the post, upwards of three-quarters of an hour being cut to waste by the refractory behaviour of the jockeys.' This behaviour cost Wyatt and Hardy fines of five sovereigns, and Mordan and Jarvis forked out two sovereigns each.

There followed a four-horse race and a two-horse match, both of which passed without too much ado. At 7 o'clock, Mr Verrall had responsibility for only one more race, the Scurry Welter Handicap, in order to see through the race meeting. Eleven runners went to the post for a 5-furlong race which wouldn't take long to run ... provided a start could be made.

Marcus Verrall did his best for an hour. The *Racing Calendar* gives us the official verdict: '... owing to the determined misbehaviour of most of the jockeys, the horses could not be got together sufficiently near to start them properly, and the race became void in consequence.'

The course stewards reported the jockeys' misbehaviour to the Jockey Club – 'the conduct of the jockeys was simply disgraceful throughout the meeting' – and recommended that adequate punishment was inflicted on Deacon and Ducker, 'the two principal delinquents'. These two jockeys received severe punishments. They were suspended for over six months (until the end of 1871) by the Jockey Club and then until 1 May 1872 by the Committee of the Grand National Hunt.

A ONE-HORSE RACE
CHELMSFORD, JUNE 1875

When does a race between two horses become so one-sided that it is no longer a race, merely a formality?

There are countless examples of one-horse races, even in recent years. The Grove Steeplechase at Doncaster in November 1971, for instance, was fought out by *Dad's Lad* and *Fairy Music* over 3¼ miles. *Dad's Lad* was so much the superior horse that odds of 1–20 were in place at the off. This was eventually returned as 'no betting' because, with the necessity of Betting Tax, the backers had no chance of winning. Betting rules stipulate that both parties should have a chance to win when the bet is made.

An earlier example of a one-horse race, probably the classic example, came at Chelmsford in 1875. The last race of Wednesday 30 June, the final day of the meeting, was The Queen's Plate, a 100-guinea race over 2½ miles. Mr H. Saville's *Lilian*, a six-year-old, and therefore carrying 10st 2lb (64.4kg), had won the Queen's Plate by 12 lengths at 15–100 the previous year, beating three other horses. Making up the field was Mr H. Augur's *Floreo*, a five-year-old carrying 10st (63.5kg). Nobody in their right mind would have bet against *Lilian*.

The instructions to J. Goater, riding *Lilian*, must have been simple. Something like 'Get back as soon as you can' or 'Don't be frightened of winning by too much'. Whereas Mr Coe, up on *Floreo*, probably heard something to the effect of 'Get back if you can' or 'No need to rush home'.

It had rained steadily throughout the day, and 'sport was rather tame'. It is unlikely that many spectators stayed to see the one-horse race at the end of the day. *Lilian* took the lead as expected, to the stand the first time round, then indulged *Floreo* with the lead for a short while. At the top turn, *Lilian* took over and drew away from her opponent, further and further and further away.

All of which added up to the strangest one-sided entry in *Racing Calendar*: 'No betting. Won by 100 lengths.'

What d'you reckon, bad handicapping?

But a word of caution is needed. It concerns the 4p.m. race at Chepstow on 28 June 1947. *Glendower*, ridden by Gordon Richards, was 1–20 to beat *Markwell* in a two-horse race. They were under starter's orders and, as the tape went up, *Glendower* dug in his toes and unseated Richards. While the 1–20 shot bounded wherever he wanted to, Gordon Richards walked humbly back to the paddock, and Mr T.R. Jones took *Markwell* on slow gallop down the 1½-mile course to win an unexpected victory.

Nothing is certain in racing. Not even one-horse races.

THE BARD WILL WALK IT

GOODWOOD, JULY 1886

'Who do you fancy for the Goodwood Cup?'

'*The Bard*'s so much better than the rest. He'll walk it.'
And that is exactly what the horse did.

In the 19th century, indeed for much of the 20th century, the Goodwood Cup rarely attracted a big field. In nine of its first 13 years, the race for the Cup fell through, and in 1826 *Stumps* walked over. But by the 1880s, the race had a rich pedigree which included the only appearance in Britain of *Kincsem*, the 1878 Goodwood Cup winner, a famous Hungarian mare who won 54 races out of 54 outings, and the culmination of the brilliant career of *St Simon* with the Cup in 1884.

Then came 1886.

The race enticed 14 entries in the first instance, but *The Bard*, son of *Petrach* and *Magdelene*, was the outstanding horse among them. 'Whatever goes to the post there is nothing to beat *The Bard*,' wrote one racing correspondent. 'I am not inclined to look beyond *The Bard* for the winner,' added another. Indeed, the favourite had won 16 races as a two-year-old.

Faced with the prospect of *The Bard*, owners gradually withdrew their horses from the Goodwood Cup. By the morning of Thursday 29 July, three runners were expected, but Mr Hammond's *St Gatien* and Lord Hasting's *Melton* were also withdrawn. That left one – Mr Peck's *The Bard*.

'The sport was bad from first to last,' said *The Times* of that day at Goodwood, '… one of the worst day's racing ever witnessed at Goodwood.'

The first race was a walk-over, the third was won by 6 lengths without trying, the fourth was a three-horse race, the Goodwood Cup was won by *The Bard*, who 'earned an inglorious pair of winning brackets by walking over', and, finally, *The Bard*, given a run in the last race, won by 10 lengths in a canter at the incredible odds of 1–9. I wonder what the watching Prince and Princess of Wales made of it all.

It was a high-class double performance from the star three-year-old, who joined the select band of horses winning two races in the same day: '*The Bard*, looking as handsome as paint, walked over for the Cup, and allowed *Whitefriar* to study the posterior position of his frame in the Singleton Plate.'

A DEUCE OF A RACE
SANDOWN PARK, JULY 1888

Ten runners went to post for the 5-furlong Surbiton Handicap at 3.45, and for two of them, *Deuce of Clubs* and *Sea Song*, their racing careers would never be the same again.

It took some time for Lord Marcus to send the ten on their way. *Wise Man* and *Sea Song* were 'fractious' at the start, but eventually they were on their journey of 5 furlongs, going almost halfway in an almost unbroken line. *Sea Song* had probably the worst start, but was soon showing with *Deuce of Clubs* as a likely horse.

As they raced for the line, three horses were in contention, *Sly Shot* being the other. But *Sly Shot* fell away, *Deuce of Clubs* 'finished like an umbrella', which presumably means he shut up very close to the end, and *Sea Song* got in a challenge in the last few strides. The result was a difficult one for the judge, and there was interim wagering on what the placings would be. Any of three had won. It was announced as a dead heat between *Deuce of Clubs* and *Sea Song*. Third-placed *Sly Shot* missed out by a head.

The winning owners could not agree to a division of the stakes, so a rerun between *Sea Song* and *Deuce of Clubs* was arranged, to take place after the day's last race. Whereas *Deuce of Clubs* had been 15–8 favourite for the original race, and *Sea Song* second favourite at 100–30, the latter now took more money and started at 8–11. Presumably the punters preferred *Sea Song*'s slow start and fast finish to *Deuce of Club*'s umbrella-closing end to the race.

Deuce of Clubs again had a better start, but after 100 yards (91.4m) *Sea Song* took up the running. *Sea Song* led for half the trip, then *Deuce of Clubs* hit back. Once again *Sea Song* came in the last few strides. Once again the result was a dead heat.

The light was good, so they tried once more. For the third heat, *Deuce of Clubs* was 5–6 favourite, but for 100 yards the two horses were 'head and head'. *Sea Song* was the first to show in front this time, but *Deuce of Clubs* took over at the 2-furlong mark. Once again *Sea Song* came with a late challenge. This time it was not quite enough. *Deuce of Clubs* won their third exciting race of the day. The distance was a neck.

It was a long, hard day for the jockeys – Liddiard on *Deuce of Clubs* and Loates on *Sea Song* – but the horses suffered the most. According to one report, both horses were 'soured for racing afterwards' but this seems an exaggeration, even though *Sea Song* tried to make a meal of Lord Abingdon's boot on a later excursion (and one presumes Lord Abingdon was wearing it at the time). After the double dead heat, *Sea Song* won only one of his next 21 races, but he continued to be pushed very hard. Although *Sea Song* and *Deuce of Clubs* were both five-year-olds when they ran their double dead heat, the former ran 71 times afterwards, the latter only 20 times.

There are earlier examples of horses being put through three races to force a decision. These include the Maiden Plate for Two Year Olds at Newmarket's Houghton meeting in 1871, when *Curtius* and *Marquis of Lorne* twice dead-heated before *Marquis of Lorne* won by a neck, and the Stonehenge Plate at Salisbury in 1867, when *Lady Barbara* and *Hue and Cry* raced three times, *Lady Barbara* winning the third quite comfortably. At Epsom, in 1873, *Arcesilaus* won the 5-furlong Durdans Selling Stakes from *Cranbourne* by 2 lengths at the third attempt. Six years after the battle between *Deuce of Clubs* and *Sea Song*, *Pippin* beat *Halsbury* after a double dead heat at Paisley, while, in 1858, in the Revival Stakes at Chesterfield, *Vatican* and *Lustre* ran two dead heats before *Vatican* walked over the course to win at the third attempt.

FOSTON FOGGYDOM

DERBY, NOVEMBER 1889

'Foggydom is beginning to assert itself, and though old Sol struggles bravely against the enemy, it cannot be expected that he can make much of a fight in his winter quarters against his terribly aggressive foe.'

They dared to race at Derby on Wednesday 13 November.

Conditions were farcical but the stewards worked their way through the whole card. Inevitably there was a mishap. It came in the day's second race, always potentially the most dangerous as it was run on a circular rather than straight course. It also took place when 'foggydom' was at its most assertive.

The day's sport began at 1p.m. with the Quorndon Plate on the straight. Visibility was less than 50 yards (45.7m) and journalists had to rely on jockeys for a description of the race. By the second race, the Foston Selling Plate, visibility had decreased.

The stewards took a few precautions to help the nine jockeys. They stationed a long line of policemen around the course to give the jockeys something to aim between. Policemen blew whistles to warn the crowd (and the other policemen) when jockeys and horses were passing them. It was some indication of where the race had reached.

In those days the Derby racecourse was a Mecca of all Derby sports. On the same site, Derby County played First Division football, Derbyshire played first-class cricket and horse racing's finest gathered. It was an open, exposed setting, attractive to all the raw elements – wind, rain or fog.

All went well in the Foston Selling Plate until about 6 furlongs from home. But not until much later was the full story unravelled. At the time all that was known for sure was that the whistles had stopped.

Six furlongs out *Domina Sylva*, the leader, went wrong in the fog. The rest of the field followed. They wandered out of the course and across the cricket ground until they were round the back of the cricket pavilion. At full racing speed, still in a bunch, they ran straight into a set of black hoardings. They were so far off the course that their cries were inaudible through the thick fog.

Watts, riding the leading horse, ended up clinging to the hoarding's palings, his arms badly scratched, while another jockey, Halsey, was unseated but unhurt. Mornington Cannon's mount, *Rappee*, ploughed through the barrier and left his 16-year-old rider behind, hanging up in the wreckage.

Fortunately, no one was badly hurt. Four jockeys did their best to steer their horses back towards the circular course. After a long delay, the noise from policemen's whistles was heard again, and a dull, muffled thump of horses' hooves once more came through the fog to the ears of 'spectators'.

Cromatie (5–1) reached the winning-post first, beating *Armada* (7–2) by a neck. *Eversfield* came in third. But Mr Clayton, acting on behalf of Lord Penrhyn, owner of one of the horses put out of the race by the hoardings, quickly lodged an objection. The horses must have taken the wrong course. The stewards listened to the evidence from the jockeys and then declared the race void.

In that instance, the stewards had a relatively easy decision to make. In a race at another foggy venue – Brighton in August 1839 – the stewards made *two* interesting decisions. First they gave the race to *Ratsbane*, overruling an objection that the horse had gone the wrong side of a post. But an hour later, another jockey, Toby Wakefield, turned up with a long story about how his horse *Tawny Owl* was the only one to go the right side of the post but had bolted at the winning-post to finish in a village a few miles away. It had taken him an hour to find his way back in the fog and now he claimed the race, For some reason the stewards gave it to him. Perhaps they went out and examined hoof-prints and matched them with the horses, as happened from time to time in the days before video evidence.

'A SINGULARLY SENSATIONAL AFFAIR'

PLUMPTON, DECEMBER 1892

The Ovingdean Steeplechase was described as 'a singularly sensational affair' and – it certainly was. The events are probably beyond the ken of modern-day horse racing enthusiasts – the rules have changed – but they really happened at Plumpton on 17 December 1892.

Three horses came under starter's orders, and there was little doubt about who would win. Mr Reeve's *Sea Wall*, ridden by Mr Atkinson and· carrying a 9lb (4.1kg) penalty for previous successes, started as 1–5 favourite. Mr Godson's *Arran* (Mr Gale up) was at 6–1, while the complete outsider was the 20–1 *Covert Side*, an aged horse owned by Mr Poole and ridden by Mr Thompson.

Covert Side 'showed a partiality for walking on his hind legs' and as soon as Mr Thompson mounted it was obvious the outsider would give him a difficult ride. It was a miracle he wasn't a faller in the paddock. *Covert Side* reared so far backwards at one point that he looked like toppling over the paddock rails. Somehow Mr Thompson coerced the horse to the start.

The Ovingdean Steeplechase was a 3-mile race over Plumpton's 'new course'. *Covert Side*, not surprisingly, was the first showing an unwillingness to cover the full distance. The horse took to jumping as a fish takes to land, and, after a mile of the race, Mr Thompson's mount stopped and did some more walking on his hind legs. The other two animals went on ahead, and *Covert Side*'s jockey lost both patience and interest in the race. Mr Thompson rode *Covert Side* back to the paddock and gave him what was variously described as 'a real leathering' and 'a regular rib-roasting'. When they reached the paddock, Mr Thompson was glad to part company with the horse.

The two-horse race was now proving eventful. Over a mile from home *Arran* fell. The poor horse was shattered. The jockey got him going again but *Arran* fell at the next too, and was completely out of the race.

That left the odds-on favourite *Sea Wall*, predictably alone. Half a mile from the winning-post he approached an open ditch ... and stopped. *Sea Wall* would go no further. His jockey tried and tried again. *Sea Wall* refused and refused. The favourite's backers waved carrots but the horse would have none.

Whatever you say about bookmakers, they can think quickly at times like this. There was no profit in a void race, there were heavy losses if the 1–5 *Sea Wall* started jumping again, but what if the 20–1 outsider *Covert Side* came out of the paddock and took up the race again?

'Come on, Mr Thompson, get back on your horse.'

By this time, *Covert Side* had quietened down and was no longer doing hind-leg stands. Mr Thompson remounted, took *Covert Side* back to the mile marker and resumed jumping.

The bookmakers were taking some risk in encouraging this new turn of events. Some punters were still backing *Sea Wall* on the principle that the favourite would wait for a horse to jump the open ditch and then set off after him. But it wasn't to be. The beaten *Covert Side* – beaten in both senses – jumped everything and *Sea Wall* still refused. Mr Thompson took *Covert Side* home alone ... and how the bookmakers in the ring cheered.

Some people argued that the race should be void, but *Covert Side* had not 'exceeded his privileges'. Nowadays, though, a jockey returning to the paddock and dismounting would be disqualified. Not so at Plumpton in the 1890s in 'a singularly sensational affair'.

THE TRODMORE RACES

TRODMORE, SUPPOSEDLY
(BUT NOT REALLY) IN CORNWALL,
AUGUST 1898

On 1 August 1898, a race card for 'Trodmore Races' was printed in the *Sportsman*, a newspaper of similar standing to *Sporting Life*. There were six races on the card, and they looked well subscribed and convincing enough on paper: the 1.30 Farmers' Plate of 2 miles over hurdles, the 2.00 Hunt Hurdle Race over two miles, the 2.30 Anglian Sweepstake over 2½ miles, the 3.00 Handicap, the 3.30 Hunters' Flat Race and the 4.00 Hunt Steeplechase over 2½ miles.

Only one problem. Trodmore didn't exist.

The next day the results appeared in the *Sportsman*. There was nothing particularly abnormal about them. The six winners included four favourites and two others at reasonably short odds: *Jim* (5–4) won by 5 lengths, *Rosy* (5–1) by a length and a half, *Spur* (2–1) won 'pulling up', *Reaper* (5–1) won 'very easily', *Curfew* (6–4) by a head and *Fairy Bells* (7–4) by a distance.

Now a second problem. The races hadn't taken place.

Bets had been placed, and some bookmakers paid out on results printed in the *Sportsman*. Others preferred to wait until they appeared in *Sporting Life*, but, when that eventually happened, one winner, *Reaper*, was shown at 5–2 rather than 5–1. It was only a printer's error, but it was enough to alert suspicions, especially as *Reaper* had been heavily backed. It was quickly discovered that there was no such place as Trodmore – certainly not in Cornwall where it was rumoured to be – and only two of the 41 listed horses had an entry in the *Racing Calendar*. The rest were presumably fictitious.

It was embarrassing for the *Sportsman*, especially as their chief racing correspondent wrote under the pseudonym of 'Vigilant'. The editor had printed the racecard as it was supplied to him in person by a man claiming to be Mr G. Martin, Clerk of the Course at Trodmore. The results were telegraphed to Fleet Street by the same man. When the newspaper editor later tried to investigate a little further, a letter to G. Martin was inevitably returned as 'unknown'.

The whole scheme was a betting fraud. The Trodmore Races provided the biggest cast-iron betting certainties in history, but only for those who were in the know. Bookmakers weren't too happy at losing money on non-existent horses who had won races that didn't take place. They were a little disappointed with the normally very reliable *Sportsman* and *Sporting Life*, which highlights the vulnerable and responsible position that racing correspondents can be put in. An Australian sports editor was once arrested for conspiring to give out the time of a race as 3.30 rather than 3.00, thus enabling a group of long-distance punters to bet knowing the result of the race. The editor was released when it was discovered that he had sent the correct time to the newspaper's print-room.

The Trodmore-scheme culprits were never found – a group of Fleet Street journalists were suspected – but it is to their credit that they weren't too greedy about their fictional races. How many people could have resisted slipping in a winner at 20–1 or even 33–1?

It is also to their credit that the villains couldn't let the occasion slip past without a touch of humour. They made their money on the fourth race of the day, and they had named the winner *Reaper*.

A NATIONAL NEEDING A SPARE NECK

AINTREE, LIVERPOOL, MARCH 1901

A blizzard raged. Snow gathered on the top of the threatening fences. And visibility was very poor. It was a pretty, Christmas-card scene ... unless you had to ride in it.

Almost all the jockeys waiting for the start of the 1901 Grand National signed a petition saying that the race should be postponed. There was a delay of ten minutes, then the stewards made the strange decision that racing was possible. They told the jockeys that the race was on.

Arthur Nightingall, riding a horse called *Grudon* that day, summed up the mood of the crowd in his autobiography: 'Some of the ancient hunting men, who attend in large numbers at Aintree to see the "National", were vastly delighted. It reminded them, no doubt, of their own grand old days of derring-do when they rode after fox through snow and over tremendous obstacles just as though they had a spare neck in their pocket, and were not afraid to produce it in the nick of time.'

Not only did Nightingall need a spare neck but a spare brain. It came from his mount's owner and trainer, Bernard Bletsoe, who, assessing the conditions at the last moment, bought 2lb (0.9kg) of butter and spread it into *Grudon*'s hooves to prevent the snow from balling. As soon as the race started, it was obvious to Nightingall that his horse held an advantage.

Grudon led at the first, and still led at the fourteenth.

Nobody except the jockeys could see what happened in between, and even they couldn't see much, The obstacles often weren't visible until the very last moment, which obviously resulted in some wayward jumping.

Much of the second circuit was out of sight, but Nightingall later verified that he had led from start to finish. *Grudon* gave Nightingall a minor fright in the run-in, though, when he jumped a footpath thinking it was another fence. In the conditions, the horse and jockey achieved miracles, coming home to win by 4 lengths to give Nightingall his third win in the Grand National.

In retrospect, however, the smartest horse of the era must have been *Manifesto*, who competed in eight out of ten Grand Nationals between 1895 and 1904. *Manifesto*'s claim to the title of 'brain of horse racing' must be derived from the fact that he was rested from the 1901 race, when a spare neck was needed, and injured before the 1898 race, when conditions were almost as bad. In *Manifesto*'s other eight attempts, he was ridden by four different jockeys to first place twice (1897 and 1899), third place three times, fourth once and eighth in his final attempt (1904). Only once did he fall in the big race.

A MARINE ACHIEVEMENT

NEW ORLEANS, USA, MARCH 1903

'The Crescent City Derby was the most successful marine achievement which has marked the history of New Orleans since the arrival of the dry dock and the docking of the *Illinois*.'

They expected a wet and muddy racetrack but no one could have forecast such a deluge on the day of the big race. Around 8in (20.3cm) of rain fell during the six-race meeting, and over 5in (12.7cm) between 1p.m. and 3p.m. *The Daily Picayune* reported the race as if it had taken place on water rather than on land: 'The Crescent City Derby was sailed over the Fair Grounds Course yesterday afternoon and the staunch craft *Witful*, from the Hildreth fleet, came home under double reefs half a hundred billows in front of her nearest rival. *Rosanco*, a home-built bark, got second money by two knots, while *Birch Broom* weathered the breakers over the harbor bar half a bowsprit ahead of *Embarrassment*.'

Half a gale was blowing and the clouds burst as soon as the meeting began. The conditions were probably the worst at a racecourse in the 20th century, although there are 19th-century tales of horses running belly-deep at Carlisle and through the overflown Tees at Stockton racecourse. (Incidentally, if you don't know the answer to the popular quiz question as to which is Britain's wettest racecourse, here it is – Putney to Mortlake.)

At New Orleans, in March 1903, the conditions were more suited to a boat-race than a horse race: 'The drainage ditch circling the track next to the outside rail overflowed by the time the second race was called, and there was a foot of water on the back stretch from the five-eighths pole until well into the home stretch.'

It was horses for courses, and swimmers for the later races. All the races were run in blinding rain, and the fourth race, the Crescent City Derby, was no exception. The owners' colours were indistinguishable, number cloths were blown up and jockeys lost their caps. Spectators (3,000–4,000 of them) were still able to cheer as the horses galloped a mile and a furlong through the 'sea of slush' and 'rough seas'. *Witful*, the 6–5 favourite, found as good a course as any and satisfied his supporters by coming to the front late and then winning easily.

One bookmaker, having lost heavily on *Witful*, offered even money that they would all have to swim home, but there were no takers. People quickly realised that their most likely forms of transport – the street-car system and the railroad – were badly hampered. There was so much rain that conditions became dangerous, and the racecourse stables were seriously flooded. That evening the horses were moved into the betting-ring and the paddock. With sleep impossible, the stable-lads spent most of the night trading racetrack tales. This was one occasion that Americans could not help but talk about the weather.

GREAT METROPOLITAN MISTAKES

EPSOM DOWNS, APRIL 1903

'But to cut my story short,' wrote a correspondent in the *Sporting Life*, 'a plumper goes to *Prince Florizel* who is sure to stay every yard of the course. The runners-up to the raking son of *Florizel II* may be found in *Parody* and *Wavelet's Pride*, both of whom can gallop the necessary two miles and a quarter.'

Not only was the correspondent's 'plumper' for the 1903 Great Metropolitan Stakes the wrong choice, but he also misjudged the length of the race, for this was the year that the runners needed to gallop 4½ miles rather than 2¼ miles. Yes, a big handicap race of this century had to be rerun after a major classic error.

Nine runners competed for a race worth 1,000 sovereigns. *Wavelet's Pride* had a long lead from *Liquidator*, *Grand Deacon* and *Prince Florizel*, when, reaching the junction of the old and new courses, their horses galloping at high speed, the jockeys were thrown into confusion. *Grand Deacon* and *Parody* appeared to run very wide, whereas *Liquidator* and *Prince Florizel* followed *Wavelet's Pride*. Suddenly a gap of several hundred yards opened up between the two groups of horses, with the back markers even more confused.

Wavelet's Pride won by 6 lengths from *Liquidator*, *Prince Florizel* and *Florinda*. *Parody* recovered well to finish fifth, but the horse's jockey raised an objection to the first four finishers and claimed the race.

The stewards made their statement: 'In connection with the race for the Great Metropolitan Stakes, C. Trigg, the rider of *Parody*, claimed the race on the ground that the horses who finished in front of him went the wrong course. This was not disputed, and as the judge had not placed *Parody*, the stewards decided that the race should be run again after the Banstead Plate.'

For the second race, at the end of the afternoon, the field was reduced from nine to five. The race favourite – and *Sporting Life* plumper – *Prince Florizel* was missing from the rerun, which took place so late in the day that some folk, including one or two racing correspondents, had gone home.

A new book was opened for the 'trifling betting' which took place on the track between the original misguided race and the rerun, and *Wavelet's Pride* became the new favourite. *Parody* was second favourite, and presumably favourite to take the right course.

The rerun was much closer than the first race, *Wavelet's Pride* racing neck and neck with *Parody* and just getting up to win the Great Metropolitan Stakes for the second time that day. Was this fair? Or would a win for *Parody* have been justice?

Bets were settled with the original starting prices, which saw *Wavelet's Pride* at 5–1 (for the first race) rather than 5–2 (for the second race), and, for those inclined, there was a chance to bet on what later action the stewards might take. In fact, a couple of days later, the course stewards, Leonard Brassey, Arthur James and Leopold Rothschild (acting for Lord Durham) inspected the course, and, deciding that it was incorrectly marked, fined the Clerk of the Course £50.

HOW FAR DID YOU SAY?
NEWMARKET, APRIL 1903

The Peel Handicap over the Peel Course at Newmarket was a 6-furlong race. Or it should have been.

The 12 runners provided a thrilling spectacle. *Renzo* (5–1) pipped *Set Fair* (5–1) by a head, the two horses fully justifying their equality in the betting. *Righteousness* was third at 10–1.

But wait. A protest was lodged immediately after the race.

Miller, the rider of *Set Fair*, alleged that the horses had not run the correct distance.

The Peel Course, after which the Peel Handicap was named, should have been 6 furlongs. They had started in the right place but finished wrong. And the fault lay with the judge, Mr Robinson. He had simply gone to the wrong winning-post.

The stewards fined the judge £20 and ordered the race to be rerun after the last race on the card. This time five of the original 12 runners went to the post, including *Renzo* and *Set Fair*, first and second over the wrong distance. Any extra betting caught *Renzo* as 6–4 favourite, with *Set Fair* 2–1, but the earlier starting prices would hold good for bets placed before the first race.

Renzo and *Set Fair* fought it out again. And again the distance between them was a head, only this time in favour of *Set Fair*. The most important distance, though, was that of 6 furlongs. The judge was at the correct winning-post and the result held good.

ONE OBJECTION AFTER ANOTHER

ALEXANDRA PARK, SEPTEMBER 1903

The order past the winning-post was not easy to determine, but the judge made his decision: Sir J. Blundell Maple's *Royal Minister* beat *Postman's Knock*, owned by Mr M.N. Rhodes, by a short head. Mr A. Walton's *Balada* was third past the post, and Mr W.C. Whitney's *White Webbs* fourth. Then came the objections, one after another, until there was a sequence of four.

Mr Rhodes objected to *Royal Minister* on the grounds of boring. The acting stewards, Messrs Owen and Chetwynd, sustained the objection and awarded the race to *Postman's Knock*. This was not greeted too kindly by one punter, who had over £5,000 on *Royal Minister* at 6–4.

Then came a second objection. Mr Walton and Mr Bird, acting for the owner of *Royal Minister*, objected to *Postman's Knock* in the belief that the horse carried insufficient weight. This objection was also sustained, and the race was now destined for *Balada*.

More was to follow. Mr Bird launched a further objection. He claimed that Mr Rhodes, the owner of *Postman's Knock*, had officiated at an unrecognised meeting. Mr Rhodes admitted that he had done so, but was not aware he was infringing any rules, By now the course stewards, Lord Ebury and Lord Lurgan, were back in harness – the race had been the last of the day and the objections were spilling over – and they agreed that it was a contravention of rule

178(a). They disqualified Mr Rhodes from entering or running any horse under the rules of racing.

Mr Bird then pointed out that this made the entry of *Postman's Knock* invalid, and the stewards agreed. The earlier objection made by Mr Rhodes was therefore quashed. *Royal Minister* was reinstated as the winner, one of the few horses to have won a race from which he was disqualified.

The owner of *Balada* was given leave to appeal to the Jockey Club – by this time everybody was totally confused and the punter with £5,000 on *Royal Minister* was perspiring plenty – and this he duly did. But the Jockey Club stewards upheld the course stewards' verdicts, although they weren't too happy that different stewards had tackled the different objections. The Jockey Club also withdrew the disqualification on Rhodes as they considered that he had inadvertently acted as an official at an unrecognised meeting.

The Moderate Plate for three-year-olds and upwards therefore goes down in history as one with four separate sets of placings along the way. They had arrived past the post as *Royal Minister*, *Postman's Knock* and *Balada*. The first objection brought *Postman's Knock*, *Balada* and *White Webbs*. The second objection produced *Balada* and *White Webbs*. But the final placings were *Royal Minister*, *Balada* and *White Webbs*.

It was very satisfying for the big £5,000 backer ... but imagine the stress.

TRANSPORT DIFFICULTIES

DEAUVILLE, FRANCE, 1905

If we are to believe Campbell Russell, an experienced owner, trainer and rider, writing in *Triumphs and Tragedies of the Turf*, there have been few stranger race meetings in the 20th century than one at Deauville in 1905. I haven't been able to confirm the specific details – it didn't happen at the big August Deauville meeting – but the story seems worth resurrecting anyway. Its main ingredient is a cunning piece of deception by 'Snowy' Williams, and that was only to reach the racecourse.

France was plagued by a rail strike, yet the organisers of the Deauville meeting decided to press ahead. Like nearly all the other jockeys in France, Williams was staying at Maisons-Laffitte, 10 miles (16.1km) from the centre of Paris. Deauville, on the Normandy coast, was 140 miles (225km) away by rail, and there was little other transport. The only train going to Deauville that day was the *Rapide* from Paris, an express train not scheduled to stop at Maisons-Laffitte.

'Snowy' Williams set his mind on boarding the express train somehow. He cajoled the Maisons-Laffitte stationmaster into sharing a glass or two of wine and explained that he was sure to ride two or three winners if he could get to Deauville. The stationmaster agreed to help the jockey.

Wearing the stationmaster's cap and jacket, Williams walked to Hasires, 1 mile (1.6km) up the line towards

Paris. Then, boldly, he stood in the middle of the track and waved a borrowed red flag. The *Rapide* slowed down, Williams hopped on the back and signalled to proceed. As the express picked up speed and went through Maisons-Laffitte, the jockey threw the borrowed clothes and flag on to the platform. At Deauville Williams alighted and sprinted for the racecourse while officials searched for the *chef de gare* who had boarded the train.

He was the only jockey to arrive on time.

The stewards delayed a while, then decided the racing should start. In his career Williams rode about 850 winners, but his five this day demanded very little of his skill. They were all walk-overs. He would have won the sixth and last race of the day too, but the other jockeys turned up. Williams came in third.

The railway continued its investigations into the bogus stationmaster and fined the jockey 1,500 francs for his impersonation. The fine was paid by Baron de Copen, owner of three walk-over winners at Deauville that day.

THE COUP OF THE MISSING HURDLE

CARDIFF, MARCH 1905

Ken Payne, a notorious gambling trainer of recent years, once documented a technique for setting up a coup: run a horse over the wrong distance, out of his class or over unsuitable ground, chalk up a string of zeros against his name, then pick the race he will win and scatter the money. Whether Gus Hogan used this technique is uncertain, but he knew he had a sure thing in *Tiara* at Cardiff in March 1905. He enlisted the help of Campbell Russell, and, between them, the two men had bets of £650 running on *Tiara* for the Ely Selling Handicap, a race of 2 miles.

After a one-sided match had started the day's races, six horses went to the post for the Ely Selling Handicap, and Russell and Hogan were reasonably pleased at the odds of 3–1 offered on *Tiara*. The favourite was *Ingratitude* (5–2), ridden by Ivor Anthony, a famous jockey of the day. The men working the coup weren't unduly worried.

Sure enough, *Tiara* ran very well on going described as 'just a trifle sticky', and the favourite blew up a quarter of a mile from home. At the second last, though, *Tiara* struck the hurdle and it was all jockey Rees could do to stay in the saddle. *Jovial King* slipped by, came home 3 lengths in front of *Tiara*, and Campbell Russell and Gus Hogan kissed goodbye to £650.

In the weighing-room, however, something very strange happened. Ivor Anthony informed Mr Harries, the owner of the beaten favourite, that he felt sure he had jumped only seven hurdles, whereas a 2-mile race had to have eight hurdles (six for the 1½ miles and one more for each subsequent quarter of a mile). If true, this was astonishing.

The stewards sent someone out to check the course, and Anthony was correct. The Ely Selling Race had been run with seven hurdles rather than eight. The acting stewards for the Cardiff meeting, Lord Tredegar, Colonel Lindsay, Colonel F.C. Morgan and Mr W.H. Jenkins, held an inquiry. The race was declared null and void, and an announcement made the following day.

Hogan and Russell couldn't believe their luck. *Tiara*, their 'sure thing', had lost, yet they were able to have their stakes returned because the race was null and void. Russell, however, couldn't understand why the race wasn't rerun with the correct number of hurdles later in the day. The reason was probably because the stewards initially decided to take no action in the matter. Only when they checked with the Jockey Club and reread rule 4S did they declare the race null and void.

AN ITALIAN LOVE STORY
EPSOM, JUNE 1908

Chevalier Ginistrelli, an Italian nobleman, came to Britain in the early 1880s, bringing with him a handful of ordinary race-horses. He lived at Newmarket, where he developed a reputation as an eccentric romantic, a cheery, personable man who trained his own horses and was not taken too seriously on the turf.

In 1889 Ginistrelli had some success with a two-year-old filly called *Signorina*, who won nine races that year and, more importantly, earned her owner's endearing, everlasting affection. The filly would sidle up to the Italian and nuzzle his pockets for sugar, apples and carrots. Ginistrelli fed the animal titbits and generally treated her as though she were a royal lady. Racegoers grew fond of the sight of the two of them, but *Signorina* failed as a three-year-old, winning only once.

Signorina went to stud, but was not a great success there either. She was barren for her first ten seasons before producing *Signorino*. In 1904, however, there occurred one of the great love stories of racing stables. Ginistrelli, a man with both eyes on the romantic, noticed how *Signorina* reacted when *Chaleureux* was brought back from his morning exercise. The filly would whinny softly from her paddock as the horse went past in a wooing way. Ginistrelli decided the two were made for each other. He put them together, and the result was *Signorinetta*, a filly born in the year that *Signorino* managed third place in the Derby.

Punters saw little of value in *Signorinetta*, but Ginistrelli thought the world of her. That she won only one race as a two-year-old – the Criterion Nursery at Newmarket's Houghton meeting – was somehow irrelevant to his love of the animal. That she failed to win races as a three-year-old, and came nowhere in the One Thousand Guineas and Newmarket Stakes, did not stop the eccentric Italian from entering his filly in both the Derby and the Oaks.

A crowd gathered to watch Ginistrelli box *Signorinetta* for the journey from Newmarket to Epsom.

'Gentlemen,' said the owner-trainer. 'This is the winner of the Derby and the Oaks.'

The onlookers laughed. They knew that the Italian trained his horses as best as he could, but there was no other horse in his string to give *Signorinetta* a good gallop. He had to resort to pacing his Derby horse with one animal for half the gallop and another for the second half.

'Don't laugh at me,' said Ginistrelli, good-humouredly, 'I am going to win the Derby with my pet.'

'Next week,' said one of the group. 'When all the others have gone home.'

Signorinetta really had no chance for the Derby, but Ginistrelli slept in her stable at night, just to ensure that his filly was safe for the big race. On the morning of Derby Day, newspapers listed 18 runners, and 17 were better fancied than the Italian's loved one. *Signorinetta* was listed at 1,000–9, but by the start of the race the odds had shortened a little – to 100–1. Comments about her chances were limited to the platitudes that she was the only filly in the race and had drawn number 13.

The favourites for the 1908 Derby were *Norman III*, winner of the Two Thousand Guineas, and *Mountain Apple*. One of the other fancied runners, *White Eagle*, had conceded 19lb (8.6kg) to *Signorinetta* at Sandown the previous year and had still beaten her.

On a wonderful summer's day, warm and sunny, the best that Britain could offer, the 18 three-year-olds set off on the famous trip of 1½ miles. All except *Vamose*, who whipped round and was left by 20 lengths. *Mercutio* and *Norman III* were early leaders but both were in trouble by Tattenham Corner. In the straight it was between *White Eagle* and *Mountain Apple* with *Sea Sick II* also going well.

According to *Sporting Life*, 'Suddenly, a quarter of a mile from home, it was realised that something on blue and white hoops, on the outside, was travelling as well as anything, and running on strongly.'

Responding to two strokes of her jockey's whip, *Signorinetta* went clear and won by 2 lengths.

'Men looked at each other, and could scarcely realise the startling result,' was *Sporting Life*'s further comment.

Signorinetta celebrated by taking Bullock on an extra tour of Epsom, the jockey unable to pull up the winner immediately. When the shock had subsided, supporters of the Turf began to congratulate the popular Ginistrelli, pounding his back and pumping his hand. The Italian waited excitedly for the horse to be brought in and then danced out to meet her, beaming brightly all over his face. His love-foal had become the fourth filly to win the Derby.

Two days later *Signorinetta* won the Oaks too. *French Partridge* brought down *Rhodora*, the 6–4 favourite and One Thousand Guineas winner, allowing *Signorinetta* to come home fairly easily by three-quarters of a length at 3–1.

King Edward VII sent for Ginistrelli, and the winning owner-trainer appeared in Epsom's Royal Box wearing a grey alpaca coat and an inappropriate panama hat. Regardless of Ginistrelli's lack of topper and tails, the King hailed the Italian and offered him for the crowd's applause. The crowd cheered the winner of the Derby and the Oaks, but most of all they cheered a man who loved his horses.

GLENSIDE'S YEAR
AINTREE, LIVERPOOL, MARCH 1911

Frank Mason was down to ride *Glenside*, but he fractured a leg shortly before the Grand National. The best Mason could do was hobble around the National course and make a rash prediction about the test of nerve and skill the race would demand. None of the competitors will complete the course, Mason said.

Although only five of 25 had finished the year before, Mason's prediction seemed rash for three good reasons. First, the fences all measured lower than the previous year. Second, the glut of fallers in 1910 was considered exceptional. And, third, there was the strength of the field for 1911, 26 good horses, including a good bet from France, *Lutteur III*.

The mount Mason had withdrawn from, *Glenside*, was an unusual beast with only one good eye. The horse was not a good stayer, but might have been fancied better than 20–1 had it not been for news that a throat infection was interfering with the horse's preparation for the Grand National. Jack Anthony replaced Frank Mason to provide an all-round British picture on the big day, for *Glenside* was an Irish-bred horse with a Scottish name ridden by a Welsh jockey in England.

The race took place in torrential rain, and five fell at the first fence. When they reached the water, about halfway round the course, only eight of the 26 were on their feet.

What was happening out there? Were they going too fast? Was it the weather, which wasn't that bad? Or was it just that these jockeys weren't as good as the old-timers? The previous year was no longer appearing exceptional.

Over Becher's for the second time, *Caubeen* and *Rathnally* were the leaders, with *Glenside* many lengths behind in third place. Then came an upset at the next, an open ditch. Both *Caubeen* and *Rathnally* saw a hole in the fence, caused when *Lutteur III* fell on the first circuit, so both went to jump through the hole. They collided and both fell.

A mile from home, *Glenside* was alone. Even when three jockeys remounted, one motivated by a private wager to complete the course, *Glenside* had two fences to spare. But this was a very, very tired horse.

One witness at Aintree was Adair Dighton, who recalled the finish in *My Sporting Life*: 'Watching the race from the Canal Bank Stand it was obvious that *Glenside* was a beaten horse as he came over the Canal Turn fence, but then as the field came round for Valentine's, Jack (Anthony) seemed to take him between his legs and lift him over this fence and go on to do the same over the remaining obstacles.'

Jack Anthony knew *Glenside* well, and had ridden the horse before. The jockey cajoled and encouraged the horse forward, step by step. At the last fence, *Glenside* rose sluggishly and hit the top, almost falling but not quite. The run-in was almost a walk-in, *Glenside*'s tongue hanging out of his mouth. Would he make it? Yes, just. Ten yards (9.1m) after the finishing-post, the horse stopped. The remounted *Rathnally*, full of running, was second by only 20 lengths, and had the race been 50–100 yards (45.7–91.4m) longer, *Rathnally* would have been the first remounted horse to win the Grand National. Instead, it was *Glenside*'s year, and Frank Mason's prediction that all the horses would fall had been spoiled only by the horse he was supposed to have ridden.

TINTO vs MYRIAD
ALEXANDRA PARK, LONDON, SEPTEMBER 1912

A big crowd on the Muswell Hill fields watched the Harringay Selling Plate. The field was a moderate one, but the race was amazing.

The two horses featuring in the close finish were very different. *Tinto* was a three-year-old outsider, a colt without a win in eight races as a two-year-old and eight previous races as a three-year-old. Ridden by A. Duller, *Tinto* was 10–1 for this race, and didn't seem very good value at that.

The 7–4 favourite was *Myriad*, a six-year-old gelding with a good track record. Trained by Barling at Ilsley, *Myriad* was ridden by the great Australian Frank Wootton, champion Flat jockey for four successive years (1909–12). Wootton won over 600 races in those four years alone. When he became too heavy for the Flat, after serving in Mesopotamia in the First World War, he switched to National Hunt and retained his brilliance.

These two horses, *Myriad* and *Tinto*, raced with nine others over a mile and 150 yards for the Harringay Selling Plate. A quarter of a mile from home, *Myriad* came to the front and the race looked like going to the favourite. Even when *Tinto* took the lead for a short time *Myriad* came back a furlong from home. Then Wootton seemed to ease his mount in the last furlong, and *Tinto* came with a surprising, plucky run to put up a challenge in virtually the last stride. It was a dead heat between *Tinto* and *Myriad*, with *Comique* half a length away third, while the second favourite, 2–1 *Admiral Byng* had drifted out to seventh place.

Myriad and *Tinto* ran off the dead heat, and the jockeys' tactics were virtually the same as before. *Myriad*, 2–5 for the rerun, had a clear lead until 200 yards (183m) from home, then *Tinto* came again, and another ding-dong finish was the result. Again the judge, Mr Robinson, could not separate the two horses. Another dead heat.

After 2 miles and 300 yards of no definite outcome, it was fortunate that, in the name of humanity, the race did not run to a third heat. The owners agreed to divide the stakes.

What made this a particularly strange race was the sale of the two winners after the two dead heats. The six-year-old *Myriad* fetched 360 guineas, exactly twice as much as the three-year-old *Tinto*. Perhaps the buyers hadn't really believed their eyes, or perhaps reputations didn't die with one race, or even two.

EMILY DAVISON AND A DISQUALIFICATION

EPSOM DOWNS, JUNE 1913

As the field of 15 runners approached Tattenham Corner in the 1913 Derby Stakes, hearts and minds worked overtime. The jockeys were hastily appraising their best position for the difficult corner, the horses were being asked to strain like never before, and the spectators were bobbing and weaving to catch sight of the horses they had backed.

One woman's mind was moving quicker than anyone's.

Emily Davison had a good mind, one that had brought her a first-class degree in English at Oxford University, one that had led her to conclude that women were worthy of equal status to men and at least worthy enough to vote in national elections. Now 40 years old, Emily Davison had been a member of the Women's Social and Political Union for seven years, and her campaign for women's suffrage had included several angry, attention-seeking incidents which had usually resulted in short prison sentences and her quick release after hunger strike.

Now, as the favourite *Craganour* and the 100–1 outsider *Aboyeur* literally battled their way through Tattenham Corner neck and neck, Emily Davison prepared for her most daring act. She ducked under the rails and ran across the course with her skirt trailing. Walter Earl, riding *Agadir*, steered his horse past the woman, who was now stranded on the racecourse. The next horse bearing down on her was *Anmer*, owned by the King. Davison raised her arms high as though she was going to seize the reins. The shoulder of the galloping top-speeding horse struck her on the head and threw her down, her hat flying across the course. *Anmer* fell head over heels, and jockey Herbert Jones was down on the floor, 12 yards (11m) away from Emily Davison. The horse was quickly on his feet. The humans were not.

The action took a split-second and bemused the crowd, who spread on to the course and surrounded the victims.

'What was she doing?'

'Was she trying to cross the track?'

'Did she think all the horses had passed?'

In the crowd a placard was raised. 'Votes for Women,' it said. People would soon conclude that Emily Davison's action was prearranged, although jockey Herbert Jones later spoke of a look of horror on the woman's face just before the impact. That she had been struck by the King's horse, rather than any other horse, was either a chance occurrence or an incredibly perfect piece of timing on a day that the King and Queen were both present. More likely it was the former.

Herbert Jones, *Anmer*'s jockey, was suffering from concussion and cuts and bruises. He was shaken but not seriously injured. Emily Davison was taken to a nearby hospital.

The drama of the 1913 Derby was far from over. As the crowd gathered round the fallen man and woman, still trying to fathom the meaning of the incident, the other 14 horses were within sight of the finishing-line. Much to the public's delight, *Craganour* was looking strong in an incredibly tight field. A well-bred horse, from *Desmond* and *Veneration II*, *Craganour* had cost owner Bower Ismay 3,200 guineas. Running in the Two Thousand Guineas, he had looked a winner all the way, even past the winning-post – by a length, some claimed – but the verdict had gone against him. Willie Saxby, the jockey on that occasion, was not given any further rides on the horse, a move that probably caused some ill-feeling which carried over to the home straight of the Derby Stakes.

American Johnny Reiff, brought over from France to ride *Craganour* and felt by some to be past his prime, was battling hard in the home stretch, but *Aboyeur*, a notoriously bad-tempered horse, was being steered towards him. The horses bumped clumsily, but *Craganour*, the 6–4 favourite, stayed in front and the crowd cheered him home.

Craganour's trainer 'Jack' Robinson was delighted. Then came a delay, and Robinson grew more agitated. 'There can't be anything wrong,' he mused. 'They can't be objecting.' But when *Craganour* was led towards the winners' enclosure, an official shouted 'Take him back'. The objection flag was raised in the number-board, just as Herbert Jones was carried on a stretcher through the unsaddling enclosure.

The owner and jockey of *Aboyeur* weren't objecting, but the judge had his own observations. The stewards made their shock announcement 15 minutes later: 'The stewards objected to the winner on the grounds that he jostled the second horse. After hearing evidence of the judge and several of the jockeys riding in the race, they found that *Craganour*, the winner, did not keep a straight course and interfered with *Shogun*, *Day Comet* and *Aboyeur*. Having bumped and bored the second horse, they disqualified *Craganour* and awarded the race to *Aboyeur*.'

The crowd were stunned. Later analysis suggested that a mistake had been made, but it was too late. The judge also erred in failing to spot *Day Comet* finishing fourth – presumably he was watching the jostling on the other side of the course – and, after the disqualification, the wrong horse was promoted to third place.

Four days later, after a head operation had been performed by a prominent male surgeon who supported female militancy, Emily Davison died in hospital. The inquest drew its conclusions: 'That Miss Emily Wilding Davison died of fracture of the base of the skull, caused by being accidentally knocked down by a horse through wilfully rushing on to the racecourse on Epsom Downs during the progress of the race for the Derby; death was due to misadventure.'

Although Emily Davison had talked of being the first woman to give her life for the women's movement, her death was considered to be an accident in terms of the law. Despite police warnings, the funeral procession attracted thousands of suffragette supporters to London. A petition was organised to campaign further for votes for women – 'And so she offered up her life as a petition to the King' – and Emily Davison's body was transported north to her burial ground at Morpeth.

Bower Ismay sold *Craganour* to Argentina for £30,000. Although he never ran again, having created an unenviable record – first past the post in both the Two Thousand Guineas and the Derby but not winning either – *Craganour* proved an outstanding success as a sire. *Aboyeur*, sold to Russia for £13,000, never won another race.

'HORSE STOPPED BY ARMED MAN'

ASCOT, JUNE 1913

Fifteen days after Emily Davison's adventurous, foolhardy act at Epsom, Harold Hewitt contemplated his plan in his Bloomsbury home. 'Oh! the weariness of these races,' he wrote in his diary on the morning of the race for the Ascot Gold Cup. 'If I fail in my intention to stop the Gold Cup, I hope I shall not hurt any of the jockeys. Oh! the weariness of these races, and the crowds they attract. They bring out all that is worst in humanity.'

Like Emily Davison, Harold Hewitt was 40 years old. He came from Herefordshire, had gone to school at Harrow and had graduated from Trinity College, Cambridge. An early anti-vivisectionist, a very religious man, abstainer and non-smoker, he was happier living an outdoor life abroad rather than an indoor life in Britain. He was disappointed with what he saw around him.

At Ascot racecourse, Hewitt hid in the undergrowth of a dense furze hedge on the outside of the track. He waited for the horses to approach as they ran for the Gold Cup, eight good horses bounding round the course. They were 7 furlongs from home, approaching the curve at the bottom of the course, and *Tracery* was in the lead, drawing ahead of *FitzRichard* but aware of a run being made by *Prince Palatine*, winner of the Gold Cup the previous year.

The scene was set for an exciting race ... but Harold Hewitt destroyed part of the contest. He walked calmly on to the track and threw up his arms in the manner of Emily Davison. Hewitt carried a loaded revolver in one hand and a flag of suffragette colours in the other. He stood defiantly, waiting for the leader, *Tracery*.

The previous night some of the jockeys had talked about the possibility of suffragette interference. Albert Whalley, riding *Tracery*, declared firmly that he would just drive straight at them. In reality, there was little time to do very much avoiding.

Hewitt was struck in the chest by the horse's head and thrown to the ground, the revolver flying out of his hand. *Tracery* was literally stopped in his tracks, while Whalley was hurled to safety several yards away. As *FitzRichard* ran by, the horse kicked Hewitt on the head, but *Prince Palatine* jumped over the fallen man.

Hewitt, bleeding heavily, was on the track for 10–12 minutes while an ambulance arrived. The police protected him from those *Tracery* supporters who wanted to tear off the injured man's arms and legs. Whalley was able to walk back to the paddock. *Tracery* galloped riderless in chase of the other runners.

For the second year in succession, *Prince Palatine* won the Ascot Gold Cup, while, in the next few days, Hewitt came off the critical list and entered Holloway Sanatorium, Virginia Water, expected to make a full recovery.

A WAR NATIONAL AT GATWICK

GATWICK, MARCH 1917

The idea of switching the Grand National from Aintree to Gatwick, as happened during the war years, may itself seem strange, but the events during the run-in for the 1917 War National also deserve mention.

This was the second National to take place away from Aintree, the first having proved far less taxing for the horses than the cruel course at Aintree. Only one horse out of 21 runners fell in the 1916 race, not necessarily because of easier fences but perhaps because the first and second fences at Aintree came after long runs, allowing horses to build up too quick a pace for safety. The distance of the two courses was about the same – just under 4½ miles – but whereas Aintree had three fences over 5ft (1.5m), the highest at Gatwick was the 4ft 10in (1.47m) eleventh (and 23rd).

The weather early in the afternoon of Wednesday 21 March threatened to contribute to a strange race. A snowstorm had people talking of *Grudon*'s success in 1901 … and presumably caused a local run on butter from those who remembered the trainer's treatment of *Grudon*. Though the snow delayed the second race, and threatened to postpone the National, conditions eased, and the big race went ahead. But the weather was yet to play a part.

Nineteen runners went to the post for the second War National, and 11 of them were still running when the field approached the second last fence of the course. *Ally Sloper*, the 1915 winner at Aintree, was running a waiting race, but the race looked more likely to be decided between *Chang* (11–2), *Ballymacad* (100–9) and *Limerock* (100–7).

Over the second last and it was soon apparent that W.J. Smith, *Limerock*'s jockey, had a lot in reserve. He let *Limerock* go and the horse went to the front, reaching the last fence a length or two in the lead. *Limerock* cleared the last fence without touching it. The horse looked home and dry.

At that point *Limerock* had jumped all 29 fences and covered 4¼ miles of the course. Just 300 yards (274m) of the run-in remained. The horse's backers, having tracked the mauve hoops worn by jockey Smith, were happy that money was theirs. What happened next shook them rigid.

Limerock was over the fence and into his stride. Then, unaccountably, the horse slipped to his knees, rolled over and put the jockey on the floor.

Ballymacad went on to win by 8 lengths from *Chang*, with *Ally Sloper* in third. Sir George Bullough, owner of *Ballymacad*, quickly announced that he would present the winnings (roughly £1,000) to the St Dunstan's Home for Blinded Soldiers.

The post-race talk, however, was mainly concerned with what had happened to *Limerock*, by *Rock Sand* out of *Annot Lyle*, owned by Lieutenant E.W. Paterson and trained by A. Gordon. There were two theories. Either the horse had crossed its legs and tripped itself up, or, more likely, it had slipped on a patch of ground made treacherous by the snow earlier that afternoon. Either way, it was remarkably odd.

THE WORST-EVER SPORTING DISASTER
HONG KONG, FEBRUARY 1918

Sports journalism has a habit of being flippant with some of the English language's most powerful words, perhaps referring to a favourite's defeat as a disaster, a broken collar-bone as a tragedy and supporters having heart failure if the race is close. When a large-scale disaster actually occurs, as it did at the Hong Kong Jockey Club in February 1918, it is difficult to find sufficiently strong words to describe the impact. Statistics, such as 604 killed, barely touch the surface.

The disaster occurred a few minutes after the running of a strange race. The Hong Kong Derby that day was 'one of the most sensational races ever ridden in Hong Kong'. A rank outsider, *Tytam Chief*, was left at the start, trailed last of seven horses for much of the way and then got up to win by a short head. For those who understand Hong Kong odds of the day, *Tytam Chief* was down for 11 wins and 55 places, whereas the favourite *Domino* was listed for 849 wins and 579 places.

The runners were taking their places for the China Stakes, and jockey John Johnstone was wondering if he could add to his five winners at the meeting, when tragedy struck.

The mat-sheds (the bamboo stands) collapsed 'like a pack of cards'. Then came the fire. Cooking stoves overturned and set ablaze the dried bamboo from which the stands were made. The sound of splitting timbers, followed by sight of the flames, sent police, military and navy personnel scampering across to rescue trapped people.

An estimated 3,000 people were in the mat-sheds at the time, mainly local Chinese, but also some Japanese and Portuguese. Early estimates put the number of dead at around 570, but that was updated later. The next day the Chinese came in hundreds to identify the victims.

The police statement was factual in its description: 'Between 2.55 and 3p.m. on the 26th, just as the fifth race was about to start, the west portion of the mat-shed booths near the racecourse swayed and fell down. Three or four minutes afterwards the eastern portion of the mat-shed fell down also. Some time afterwards fire broke out in the kitchen department of the booths ...'

Initially, the Jockey Club stewards, perhaps not fully recognising the extent of the damage, decided to delay the races for a couple of days. After adverse reaction they decided not to resume the meeting.

It was left to a 22-day inquiry to determine the details. 'Death was due to suffocation, the result of either the collapse of the mat-sheds or the fire or both,' concluded the inquiry team, who were asked to pass a verdict on one of the 604 victims. 'We do not attribute criminal negligence to anyone in connection with this death.'

The inquiry did result in some strong recommendations, which give some insight into the interacting causes of the disaster. Inflammable material like matting and bamboo should not be used. There should be gaps between the sheds to prevent fire spreading. The height of stands should be limited, and overcrowding prevented by safety limits. Enough exits should be provided. Firemen should be on duty at the racecourse, and there should be access to a decent water supply. Oil-lamps should be banned, and the customary cooking technique of using charcoal in a cooking chatty should be reconsidered.

The Hong Kong Jockey Club disaster is still the world's worst-ever in the history of organised sport.

A TRIPLE DEAD HEAT
WINDSOR, SEPTEMBER 1923

The triple dead heat for the Royal Borough Handicap at Windsor on 21 September 1923 had one special feature, which set it aside from other triple dead heats – it was captured on photograph by an eagle-eyed cameraman with good timing. For some years the photograph was displayed in the press room at Windsor, and visitors marvelled at the rare sight of how close three horses could finish. Many people have tried to judge the photograph of *Dinkie*, *Dumas* and *Marvex*, but the sole judge on the track could not separate the three horses on the line. Needless to say, backers of all three horses said that the horse they had backed had won quite easily.

A furlong from home, the race had reduced to *Dinkie*, *Dumas* and *Marvex*. *Dinkie* appeared to be the best placed, but *Dumas* and *Marvex* made simultaneous challenges, and they reached the winning-post in a line. Gardner, riding *Dumas*, completed a remarkable double, as he was also involved in the triple dead heat at Sandown Park in April 1915. But our anonymous photographer perhaps deserves the most credit; in the days before motor-drives and automatic wind-ons, he had done magnificently to make the most of this one shot. For some time it remained a classic.

The Royal Borough Handicap for three-year-olds started at 3p.m., and the four most fancied horses were *Dumas* (2–1), *Dinkie* (6–1), *Gabrielle* (7–1) and *Marvex* (8–1). There were 14 runners, and one account described the race as follows: '*Johnnie Crapaud* (on the left) showed the way to *Gabrielle*, *Kinnaird*, *Dinkie*, *Marvex*, *Dumas* and *Virgin Gold*, with *Gay Canopy* bringing up the rear, for 3 furlongs, when *Dinkie* went on second, just clear of *Gabrielle*, *Kinnaird*, *Marvex*, *Dumas*, *Miltiades*, and *Virgin Gold*, the whipper-in being *Heather Honey*. Entering the straight, *Gabrielle* weakened, as did *Johnnie Crapaud* a quarter of a mile from the post. This left *Dinkie* slightly in front of *Marvex* and *Dumas*, which pair joined issue at the distance, a thrilling race terminating in a dead heat for first place.'

While waiting for the judge's verdict, the bookmakers had a more complex time than for the actual race. Having established that *Miltiades* was definitely fourth, they were not only taking bets on *Dinkie*, *Dumas* or *Marvex* winning, but also bets for a triple dead heat or any of three separate double dead heats. The triple dead heat was the winner, and the stakes of the race were divided.

The 1923 Royal Borough Handicap adds to previous triple dead heats, such as the 1857 Cesarewitch at Newmarket, the 1858 Craven Plate at Salisbury and the 1880 Astley Stakes at Lewes. Other instances include a Goodwood race in August 1849, the 1858 Abbey Handicap at Shrewsbury, races at Doncaster (1869) and Newmarket (1875), the 1882 Sandown Derby at Sandown Park, when two horses of the three carried the wrong weight but the discovery was made too late for an objection, the 1896 Badminton Plate at York, the 1897 Huntingdon Plate at Derby, the 1915 Walton Selling Plate at Sandown Park, the 1924 Long Course Selling Plate at Newmarket and the 1925 Stayers' Handicap at Folkestone. A novel triple dead heat was that for second place at The Curragh in the 1947 Autumn Sprint Handicap.

There are also examples of a different kind of triple dead heat – three double dead heats in a day. The meeting at Birmingham in 1910 and the Eglinton Hunt meeting of 1906 come into this category.

ENGLAND'S BEST AGAINST AMERICA'S BEST

BELMONT PARK, USA, OCTOBER 1923

Only in America could they think of such an idea. The best horse in England against the best in the United States.

The American Westchester Association promoted the match in order to give American horse racing a needed boost. Recognising the publicity it would create, they sent a representative to England in an attempt to arrange the race. They persuaded Ben Irish, a farmer from Sawtry in Cambridgeshire, that he should send *Papyrus* to the United States. Irish, who had struck lucky with the horse's Derby win, was glad to oblige.

At stake was the equivalent of £20,000 for the winner and £5,000 for second place.

The race, scheduled for 20 October, was embroiled in complex organisation. In the days before commercial air travel, it meant a long trip by boat for *Papyrus* and his associates. The Derby winner, a stable companion called *Bar of Gold*, the trainer, a veterinary surgeon and Irish's solicitor left on the *Aquitania* on 22 September. Irish himself, suffering from a heart complaint, did not risk the journey. Steve Donoghue, the jockey selected for the big occasion, followed on a later boat. Donoghue was temporarily released from his commitments with Jack Joel after some negotiation. A replacement jockey, on stand-by, was not needed.

The American opposition was *Zev*, a horse owned by an oil-man called Sinclair. A few days before the race, which took place on a Saturday, *Papyrus* was expected to win, his hopes raised by a trial gallop which supposedly equalled *Man o' War*'s course record, but the horse's British connections were not too optimistic.

For one thing, *Papyrus* had unexpectedly failed to win the St Leger, his last race before leaving Britain. For another, there was the long trip by boat, during which time Papyrus had not left his specially constructed box. Then there was the Belmont Park course, a dirt track which would be unfamiliar to jockey Steve Donoghue. Finally, there was the rain, 10–12 hours of it on the night before the race.

On the Saturday of the race, the course was wet. Debate raged about whether *Papyrus* was wearing the right plates. And debate also raged about whether *Zev* would run or whether a replacement horse, *My Own*, would be drafted in. In the end, *Zev* started, and started as favourite.

The English horse was first away, but, in accordance with his promise to the starter, Donoghue allowed the American jockey, Earle Sande, to pull level. Donoghue had planned a waiting race for the 1½-mile course, so he then allowed Sande to go ahead on *Zev*. This was a mistake. Donoghue found himself riding into a hail of mud thrown up by the leading horse. A gap of several lengths appeared, but then *Papyrus* began to close.

The last turn was decisive. *Zev* came through clear, *Papyrus* struggled to accelerate in the difficult conditions, and the American horse stormed through to win easily by 6 lengths.

Though the result was a let-down for the British public, there was plenty of wining and dining, and the race satisfied its original purpose of giving American racing a 'shot in the arm'. The British contingent left on their long journey home confident that the story would have been different if the race had taken place on a dry British track of turf. But *Papyrus* was sold later that year, and his best racing days were over.

A GRAND NATIONAL FOR ALLISON AND GOOD

AINTREE, LIVERPOOL, MARCH 1927

The BBC, having broadcast rugby and football matches early in 1927, and having experimented unsuccessfully with the Derby in 1926, were keen to make a decent job of broadcasting a major horse race. The Grand National was an obvious choice.

The two commentators were *Sporting Life*'s Meyrick Good, who was accustomed to reading the race to the King, and George Allison, a non-racing newspaper reporter who had been involved in other BBC broadcasts. Allison would establish himself as a BBC man until 1934, when he took over as manager of Arsenal Football Club after the death of Herbert Chapman.

Allison's role in the 1927 Grand National broadcast was to describe scenes before and after the race. There was some experience of this from the 1926 Derby, when Laurence Anderson, Vera Lennox and R.E. Jeffrey had carried out a conversation among themselves as they looked around the atmosphere of tipsters, betters and racegoers. Their description of the actual race had been weak. According to one account it went something like 'Here they come ... now they're getting down to it ... he's drawing ahead ... it's sure to be *Lex* ... No, *Harpagon* ... it looks like nine, five and one.' (The winner was in fact *Coronach*, who led from start to finish and won by 5 lengths.)

This time Meyrick Good was in charge of the race, which proved an eventful one to describe. Good, nervous before the race, prepared countless facts about the participating horses, but these were not required by the BBC. His description of the race relied entirely on what he could see from the stand. Trying to forget the large audience, Good just talked to the microphone. The King, sitting next to Good, did his best not to interject too much as his voice would also be picked up by the microphone. It was impossible for Good to see everything on the course and spot all the fallers – only seven out of 37 horses finished the course – but he succeeded in sending waves of excitement into 10 million homes. Some people found the broadcast more exciting than actually attending. Good spotted the superb jump made by *Sprig* at the Canal Turn on the final circuit, sending the horse up to the leaders. The commentator later admitted to a sneaking fancy for *Sprig*, a bet on the horse and a lifetime relationship with Ted Leader, who was riding *Sprig*.

'Come on Ted,' Meyrick Good said to the microphone, as *Bright's Boy* and *Sprig* jumped the last fence, and *Sprig* was going the better. 'You'll win.' His words were sent via the Daventry transmitter to Great Britain and Ireland and parts of Europe.

The roar of the crowd drowned Good's last few sentences of commentary on the race, but *Sprig* did win – by a length though chased home by *Bovril III*, with *Bright's Boy* slipping back to third. Listeners waited patiently for the official announcement of the result to learn which horse had won.

The broadcast relied on five microphones. One in the private stand was manned by Meyrick Good, with the King at his shoulder. One hung in front of Good to pick up the cheers from the crowd. A third was stationed overlooking the paddock for George Allison to comment on the scenes before and after the race. A fourth was hung over the unsaddling enclosure in order to capture the sounds of cheering for the winner. The fifth was for interviewing the winning jockey. 'Good afternoon,' said Ted Leader, 'I'm very proud and very happy. *Sprig* gave me a wonderful ride.'

After 62 minutes on the air, from 2.30 to 3.32, the first major horse racing broadcast was declared a success. In June 1927 Geoffrey Gilbey and George Allison covered the Derby and Geoffrey and Quintin Gilbey did the St Leger later that year. The following year, there was an even more eventful Grand National to comment upon, one which merited the mantle of 'strange race' for events on the track rather than events surrounding five microphones.

FORTY-TWO RUNNERS AND ONE CLEAR ROUND
AINTREE, LIVERPOOL, MARCH 1928

The 1928 Grand National had a field of 42 runners, a record at the time. Visibility was poor, the going was very heavy, and so was the casualty toll.

The mist prevented people in the stands from seeing the main calamitous event of the race. It featured a much-fancied horse, *Easter Hero*, who was leading the field as he approached Canal Turn but jumped too soon and landed on top of the fence. As the other horses approached Canal Turn, they were faced with *Easter Hero* stuck in the fence. They slowed and bobbed and weaved, but there was a mammoth pile-up. More than half the horses were put out of the race.

The other fences weren't easy either. By the time they cleared Becher's for the second time, only five horses remained in the race. It was *Billy Barton* from *May King*, *Great Span* and *Tipperary Tim*, with *Maguelonne* trailing off in fifth place and then falling at the fence after Valentine's to leave but four.

Then *May King* fell, and, at the second last, *Great Span* lost his saddle, unseated his rider and was a goner too. Then there were two.

Coming to the last they were neck and neck. *Billy Barton*, over from America, was, at 33–1, by far the favourite. The other was *Tipperary Tim*, a 100–1 shot, later described as a 'hopeless scarecrow' with a 'terrible racing record'. At the last they rose together, with the riderless, saddleless *Great Span* jumping through the gap between them. *Billy Barton*, ridden by Tommy Cullinan, hit the top of the fence and came down. A noisy, American-sounding groan erupted from the stands.

That left only the outsider, *Tipperary Tim*, a horse bred in Ireland and named after a local marathon runner called Tim Crowe. *Tipperary Tim*, trained in Shropshire, was ridden by Billy Dutton, a Cambridge graduate who was articled to a Chester solicitor. Dutton, who later gave up the law to ride, made his reputation by completing the only clear round in the 1928 Grand National, though *Billy Barton*, remounted by Cullinan, came in to finish second. No other horse troubled the judge.

The purists were outraged at the idea of a mediocre horse winning the National solely by avoiding mishaps round the course, but Dutton deserved a lot of credit for adopting his tactic of riding *Tipperary Tim* wide on the outside of the course to avoid interference. The Canal Turn obstacle was converted from an open ditch to a plain fence before the next year's race, which attracted a staggering field of 66 runners, trainers and owners having been much encouraged by an outsider's win. The 1929 race was won by another 100–1 shot, *Gregalach*, from gallant *Easter Hero*, who spread a plate. *Tipperary Tim*, still 100–1, was one of 56 failing to complete the arduous course. In fact, between 1911 and 1933 only 115 out of 535 (21.5 per cent) of horses completed the National course at Aintree, and some of those had been remounted. Perhaps one clear round out of 42 wasn't so strange after all.

ENGINE-POWER AGAINST HORSE-POWER

CHICAGO, AUGUST 1933

The original race was staged in 1830, when the first locomotive built in America raced against the Pioneer horse-drawn carriage. The same two modes of transport met again over a hundred years later. The result was the same. The organisers meant it to be.

The first race took place on 25 August 1830 over a 13-mile course. It was set on Illinois Central Railroad tracks, between Baltimore and Ellicott's Mills. The *Tom Thumb* locomotive ran into mechanical difficulties, and the horse was able to storm through for a sensational victory. But it wasn't enough to halt the eventual swing in the transport system. The train won that battle.

The rerun was staged by the Baltimore and Ohio Railroad Company. The course – from 35th Street to 39th Street – was much shorter than the original course, but the result was the same. The restored *Tom Thumb* again finished second to the horse (a different horse), and backers of the locomotive would have been justified in calling for a dope test.

Horse-train races are examples of races which suggest changes in American society. Another example took place in November 1932, in Burlington, New Jersey, when a motorised fire engine raced a team of ice-wagon horses who were dragging an old-fashioned steam fire engine. The race was scheduled for one block.

The ice-wagon horses – lent to the fire company for the occasion – started very quickly and bounded into an early lead, their 40-year-old steam engine clattering on behind. What an upset. The motorised fire engine, slow to start, was still behind when they had raced a block. 'Carry on,' the organisers said. 'Go another block.' Yes, go until the motor vehicle takes the lead, which, of course, it did.

Given the horses' brilliant early start, the idea of keeping the horses in case there was a fire less than a block away was put forward but was not heeded.

Gradually, the horse has diminished in importance as a form of transport, commercial and private. Yet there are arguments in its favour. Many old-time milkmen argue convincingly for the benefit of the horse over modern electric vehicles. 'You can't whistle a milk float,' one said, when explaining how he used to get round quicker with his horse. There are still plenty of races horses can win against other forms of transport.

A RECORD FOR A 7-FURLONG COURSE

SAN FRANCISCO, CALIFORNIA, OCTOBER 1938

Twelve-year-old *Blackie* completed the 7-furlong course in a record 23 min 15 sec. This may not seem a fast time on most racecourses, but this was no ordinary 7-furlong course. It was across the entrance to the Golden Gate Bridge, through the water of San Francisco Bay. The horse took on an Olympic swimmer and swam to a comfortable victory. Very few thought he would.

One of the disbelievers was a course official of the Bay Meadows racetrack, who bet Arthur Watson, the horse's owner, that *Blackie* couldn't beat Frank Brissette. The horse not only beat the man, but knocked over a minute off the previous Golden Gate record. This had stood since 1914, when an Olympic champion, Buster Olds, had swum across. Unlike the human swimmers, *Blackie* was forced to carry a jockey, Ritchie 'Shorty' Roberts, who simply held on to the horse's tail 'cavalry' style. One newspaper engaged Roberts in a post-race interview, and *Blackie*'s trainer-rider allegedly said, with delightful ambiguity, 'The horse gave me a swell ride'.

The race across the Bay started with *Blackie* being lowered from a fishing vessel called the *Walter Paladini*. Brissette and *Blackie* swam side by side for more than half the course, which started from Line Point in Marin County and ended on an imaginary line off Fort Point. Using his improvised 'dogpaddle crawl', *Blackie* wore down the

Olympic swimmer and not only won but also showed off by swimming another half-mile or so. When the horse eventually opted to swim ashore, he had been in the water for about 40 minutes. The hero was greeted by his owner, by the losing sportsman (who immediately congratulated the horse with a bag of oats) and by movie-makers looking to sign up the horse for a few stunts.

The closest link between swimming races and organised horse racing comes in the form of picnic races on the beach, possibly the most famous being those at Laytown in Ireland. Laytown Races take place in July or August – depending on tides – and it helps if a horse is prepared for water, just in case the incoming tide interferes with the last races on the card. 'So unusual is the setting for this meeting,' wrote the *Drogheda Independent* one year, 'that scores of people, who could hardly distinguish a jockey from a "bookie", annually patronise this event and thoroughly enjoy their day's outing.'

ONE FROM THE BACK
CHELTENHAM, MARCH 1939

A book on strange races cannot be complete without at least one example of a type of race based on fantasy, a scenario capable of thrilling all people, whatever their interest in horse racing. A horse comes from the back and makes up an incredible amount of ground to win spectacularly.

This example is taken from an important 2-mile hurdle race. The 1939 Champion Hurdle at Cheltenham saw a field of 13 horses, the race's largest field at that time. As they entered the home stretch, the race was being fought out by the half-dozen front runners. *Solford*, owned by the eccentric Dorothy Paget, was battling away with the grey *Bahuddin*, with *Mask and Wig* and *Free Fare* tucked in behind, and *Vitement* and *Apple Peel* looking the best of the trailing bunch.

At the rear was *African Sister*, a comparative outsider at 10–1 and surely out of the race. Trained by Charles Piggott and ridden by Keith Piggott, Lester's father, *African Sister* had had a difficult year after suffering serious internal injuries from a fall at Wolverhampton. The horse was nursed night and day, until eventually it was racing again and considered fit enough for the Champion Hurdle. Piggott was accustomed to riding the horse from behind, but last in the home stretch was ridiculous. Then fate conspired to produce an extraordinary ending to the race.

Solford, going better than any, fell at the last. *Bahuddin*, under pressure from the whip, also fell at the last, in an unrelated incident. *Mask and Wig* swerved to avoid the two fallen horses but collided with *Free Fare*, and they both came down. That left *African Sister*, bowling along from the back, coming out of the trailing bunch, tearing through into the lead, going on to win by 3 lengths – a win for the horse from the back.

Vitement, a 20–1 shot, came in second, half a length ahead of *Apple Peel*, placed third at 100–8.

THE GOLDEN APPLE

HURST PARK, MAY 1939

After the inauguration of the Golden Apple race at Hurst Park, Percy Swaffer wondered where it would all end. It provoked him to write: 'If this touch of segregation extends, in due course we may get a Bachelors' Derby, a race for red-headed trainers and, more exclusively still, another for jockeys who don't swear.'

The Golden Apple was a race for three-year-olds and upwards. The unusual entry requirement was that, in the five weeks between the entry closing-date (25 April) and the race date (29 May), the horses had to be the property of 'a lady or ladies'. It was an iota of recognition of the role played by women in racing, albeit on a segregated basis.

By this time, women owners had enjoyed some success. Lady James Douglas was the owner of *Gainsborough*, winner of the substitute New Derby Stakes at Newmarket in 1918, plus the Two Thousand Guineas and the St Leger in the same year. Mrs Peel owned *Poethlyn*, War National winner at Gatwick in 1918 and Grand National winner a year later. *Sprig*, the winner of the 1927 Grand National, had been bequeathed to Mrs Partridge on the death of her son Richard in the First World War. And the first success for women owners in the Epsom Derby came in 1937, when *Midday Sun*, owned by Mrs G.B. Miller and her mother Mrs Talbot, pipped *Sandsprite*, also owned by a woman, by a length and a half.

When entries for the 1-mile Golden Apple race were welcomed, a respectable list of 16 horses was compiled. The owners were mostly married women – 13 out of 16 – and, of the horses, three were aged three years and three were six-year-olds. The three-year-old, 6–1 favourite *Lover's Fate*, won the race by 2 lengths. The winning horse, owned by Mrs Thurston, the wife of a Berkshire engineer, was ridden by Dave Dick and was trained in the Templeman stables. The second-placed *Frivolous Friar* was owned by Mrs A.H. Williams, and third-placed *Cordon Rose* was owned by Mrs H.P. Holt.

SPECTATORS AS JOCKEYS
HASTINGS, NEW ZEALAND, JUNE 1939

Welcome to the Napier Park Racing Club's Winter Meeting at Greenmeadows. The date is Monday 5 June and spectators are looking for some action from the Park Steeplechase, the fourth race of the day. Only four runners, and the trip of 2½ miles will probably seem a long way for all of them. *Wykemist*, a black gelding by *Royal Stag*, is ten years old but lightly raced and must have a chance. *Kikiroki* is not a bad horse either, but there is little hope for the two outsiders, *Begorrah* and *The Tramp*.

The first circuit was negotiated safely by all four runners. Then *The Tramp* fell at the stand double. At the fourth fence along the back of the second circuit, *Begorrah* lost his rider. That left *Kikiroki* a long way in front, 15 lengths clear of *Wykemist*.

Kikiroki had the race sewn up. Only 3 furlongs to run and a couple of fences to jump. But anything can happen in racing, and *Kikiroki* hinted at this by unseating his rider at the next jump. So, five minutes and 29 seconds after starting the race, *Wykemist* came home alone to win his owner, Mr D.A. Preston, the staggering sum of £135.

What happened next was weird. Rarely have spectators become so involved in a race.

First an onlooker named Mr Marquand caught up with *Kikiroki*, mounted him and took him back to the second to last fence. Marquand rode *Kikiroki* into second place.

Further back there was even more excitement. *Begorrah*, after following *Wykemist* riderless to the winning-post, had been claimed by a second spectator-cum-jockey and taken back to do a leisurely final circuit of the course. But connections of *The Tramp*, seeing this from the birdcage (the ring in front of the weighing-room where jockeys mount horses), encouraged their own jockey to remount and ride another circuit. A thrilling race for third place began, won by the spectator on *Begorrah* by a head with the crowd cheering the contest.

The stewards ratified the result – the spectator/riders had to weigh in of course – and allowed the owners to collect their share of the stakes. The owner of second-placed *Kikiroki* benefited by £30 and *Begorrah*'s owner by £10.

So, just to recap on the result of the Park Steeplechase: first was *Wykemist* ridden by E. Deslandes; second was *Kikiroki* ridden by J. Dooley and Mr Marquand; and third was *Begorrah* ridden by E. Leckie and Mr Greene.

GOING SOLO IN THE KIPLINGCOTES DERBY

ETTON TO MIDDLETON-ON-THE-WOLDS, MARCH 1947

'Few people have heard of the Kiplingcotes Derby,' writes Alison Ellerington in her book *The Kiplingcotes Derby*, 'even fewer people will have stood with their backs to the biting March wind, waiting for the first speck to appear over the horizon, gradually growing in size until horse and rider may be clearly recognised and cheered up to the winning-post.'

If you happen to visit North Humberside on the third Thursday in March, take a trip to the road between Etton and Middleton-on-the-Wolds and, even today, you will be able to witness England's oldest race, the Kiplingcotes Derby. It is run with all its original 16th-century eccentricities: the 4½-mile course of roadside grass; the weighing scales at the finish rather than at the start, forcing jockeys to ride an extra 4½ miles to the start; the reading of a shortened version of original rules before the race starts; the carrying of extra weight on the person rather than in a weighted saddle-cloth; and the strange prize money distribution – interest on the fund for first place, the pounds from entry fees for second place and the loose change from entry fees to the Clerk of the Course and the judge. If the field is a large one, second prize is more valuable than first.

In 1947 – 428 years after the race was first run – the tradition of the Kiplingcotes Derby was kept alive by 36-year-old farm hand Fred Stephenson, who rode solo over a snow-buried course in one of its most difficult years. I say 'one of' because there is evidence that, in the 19th century, some contestants had to cope with seven- or eight-feet snowdrifts, whereas in 1947 the drifts were only three to four feet deep.

In places, Stephenson was forced to dismount, clear a path and lead his horse through. The race normally takes about 10 minutes, but Stephenson's challenging ride kept him out for an hour and 20 minutes. He set off alone and came home alone, the judge waiting patiently in the cold for his return. Rarely has a walk-over been more difficult and, for his pains, Fred Stephenson won a little over £5 (the interest on the invested money) and the return of his £4 entry fee. Together with his horse, *Londesborough Lad*, he completed a hat-trick by winning the Kiplingcotes Derby in 1948 and 1949 too.

Fred Stephenson, however, could not compete with the prolific success of Frank Simpson in one of Britain's other historic races – the Newmarket Town Plate, run over 4½ miles on Newmarket Heath. Established by King Charles II in 1666, the race was won 17 times by Simpson, who competed as a 75-year-old in 1945. The Newmarket Town Plate is also significant as an early arena for women to display their riding ability. Eileen Joel was the first woman to win the race, Iris Rickaby (Lester Piggott's mother) won it twice and Audrey Bell had three successes in the 1930s – all at a time when women were barred from racing under Jockey Club or National Hunt rules.

DIVIDED HIGH STAKES
GOODWOOD, JULY 1949

In the middle of the 20th century, Turf officials around the world were relishing the value of a brilliant new idea. A camera, stationed five feet from the ground on the finishing-line, could record the horses passing the post, making the judge's job so much easier. This would solve all possible debates about close finishes.

Or would it?

Goodwood had a camera in place for the 3.45 Bentinck Stakes on Wednesday 27 July, a race over a mile and 6 furlongs. There were four runners, the favourite *High Stakes* giving a lot of weight to *Hornet III*, *Flush Royal* and *Royal Drake*. The race had a thrilling finish and an even more thrilling interpretation of the photograph.

The French horse, *Hornet III*, owned by M. Nicot, trained by Joseph Lieux and ridden by Rae Johnstone, looked a winner in the home stretch, but Gordon Richards, riding *High Stakes* for Lord Astor, came with a late, well-timed run and looked to have caught *Hornet III* on the line. It was a close-run thing, but fortunately there was the new device to decide what would have undoubtedly have been a dead heat in the days before the camera.

While spectators were betting on the outcome of the judge's decision, Malcolm Hancock studied a rushed, fuzzy print. He gave his verdict. The winner was *High Stakes*. The other high stakes, £1,295 and five shillings, would go to Lord Astor.

Then other people at the track began to study the photograph. They could see that Gordon Richards's body was in front of Rae Johnstone's, and they could see that *High Stakes*'s quarters and tail were in front of those of Hornet III, but where exactly were the horses' noses? It looked more like the nose of *Hornet III* on the finishing-line, whereas that of *High Stakes*, recognisable by a white tip, was in the air, perhaps an eighth of an inch (0.3cm) short of the line. The crowd might have turned nasty had the result not been to the favourite's advantage. Stands have been burned down for less.

Meyrick Good captured the scene for *Sporting Life*: 'The crowds made way for Gordon Richards to see the photo-finish before he left the course. The champion, with a broad wink, said: "It's a near thing."'

Later, the stewards of the Goodwood meeting agreed unanimously that *Hornet III*, rather than *High Stakes*, had reached the line first. They referred the matter to the Jockey Club, where the stewards, also studying the photograph, agreed that *Hornet III* had in fact beaten *High Stakes* but they did not have the power to reverse the judge's decision. The trainer of the French horse, Joseph Lieux, knew he would have no hope with an appeal.

In a sporting gesture, however, Lord Astor wrote to the French owner, M. Nicot, and offered half the winnings. Lord Astor made it clear that he was accepting the judge's decision and was not suggesting this should be a precedent. It was merely a private arrangement. Not much help for punters with money on *Hornet III*, of course, but perfectly acceptable to the French owner … once the tax man had established whether it was earnings or a gift. Meanwhile, *High Stakes* would be credited with the 'victory' in a career record which eventually totalled 34 wins.

All that remained was for people to debate whether photo-finish cameras had any real future. Surely, some argued, it would have been better to have given a dead heat rather than get the result wrong. Others pointed out that there would always be problems with camera angles, tricks of light, slopes in the ground and hollows in the turf. The camera could lie ... or could break down. Nor did the introduction of cameras rule out the possibility of dead heats, as was shown on 24 October 1947, when a Doncaster judge studied the photograph and ruled a dead heat between *Resistance* and *Phantom Bridge*. And, as recently as April 1986, a judge at Hereford erred on what was a very complicated photograph to interpret.

The arguments against the photo-finish camera were generally soon overcome, and more sophisticated methods were introduced, but I must mention one idea which seems to have been lost since. A *Sporting Life* reader pointed out that the problem really stemmed from relying on which nose crossed the line first. He thought he had a better idea – why not go by the horses' ear alignment?

If you agree with this, please don't write to me.

A WAITING RACE

BIRMINGHAM, AUGUST 1949

Two horses went to the post for the Midland St Leger Trial Stakes, a race of a mile and 5 furlongs, and both jockeys listened to orders. Noel Murless, trainer of *Ridge Wood*, gave Gordon Richards specific instructions not to make the running. Dick Perryman, trainer of *Courier*, told Tommy Lowrey to ride a waiting race and let *Ridge Wood* make the running.

It must have been clear to each jockey what the other intended. When the tapes went up to start the race, neither horse made a move forward. In fact, Tommy Lowrey's *Courier* actually turned round, and people watching from a distance assumed it must be a false start.

The starter shouted for the two jockeys to move forward. Then he sent his assistant across to crack his whip behind the two horses (without touching either of them). This got them moving. *Ridge Wood* and *Courier* both broke into a trot, and eventually a slow canter, both jockeys riding to orders, both resisting the opportunity to take the lead.

The horses were keen to gallop, but the two jockeys worked hard to restrain them. Gordon Richards, in what proved to be his 22nd year as champion Flat jockey (and his second most productive in terms of winners), was riding brilliantly to control his mount, sitting upright on *Ridge Wood*, the 2–5 favourite. The crowd didn't like it. They began to jeer.

The two horses travelled the first furlong in 1 min 24 sec, the average time for a complete 7-furlong race. It was not until the 6-furlong mark that the two-horse field broke into a slightly quicker canter. *Courier* was forced to the front, against Lowrey's wishes.

Three furlongs from home it almost turned into a real race. Gordon Richards made his effort on *Ridge Wood*, and for a brief moment it looked as though the two horses would race competitively all the way to the finishing-post. Then *Ridge Wood*, soon to win the St Leger, came away to win easily by 3 lengths.

As Gordon Richards unsaddled after his win – he was averaging more than two wins a day at the time – there was a most peculiar event. The crowd were actually booing the winning jockey, a man who was indisputably the best jockey of the past two decades, a man whose character and personality had commanded universal respect and who would soon be knighted by the Queen for his services to racing. And he was only riding to trainer's orders.

The time for the race was 5 mins 14 sec – more than double the expected time for a race of a mile and 5 furlongs. The local stewards spoke to both jockeys and accepted that they were merely following their trainers' instructions.

It was not the first time that Gordon Richards had been involved in a 'slow race' and far from the only occasion that a race has been run in that way. In 1933, Richards rode *Colorado Kid* against Michael Beary on *Nitsichin* in a duel for the Doncaster Cup.

John Fairfax-Blakeborough, in *Analysis of the Turf*, recalls an occasion at Blackpool early in the 20th century when two jockeys had orders to let the other lead over the first fence and the water-jump. On hearing the word 'Go', the two jockeys stayed put, then urged their horses forward into a walk. When they reached the water-jump, each still intent on letting the other go first, they were travelling too slowly to take the obstacle and both toppled in.

Fairfax-Blakeborough also has a story about a starter at Winchester, who set off a 'slow race' and was able to ride his own hack so that he could wait for the jockeys at the winning-post.

THE FERNIE-CHASE CHASE

LEICESTER, FEBRUARY 1953

The 4.15p.m. race at Leicester on Tuesday 10 February had all the perfect ingredients to provide a setting for a strange, calamitous race. The weather had been poor all day, and by the time of the Fernie Chase, the last race of the day, the course had been ploughed up and the going was very heavy. As it was a race over 2 miles for horses who had never previously won a race, anything could happen ... and it certainly did.

All three runners fell very early in the race. Thereafter it was a matter of who could chase their horse the fastest in order to bring it back on to the course.

It was a wonder that the race took place. Derby, 30 miles (48.3km) away, had 3–4in (7.6–10.2cm) of snow, and Leicester itself had been blessed with heavy rain for much of the meeting. Nevertheless, three horses went to the post to contest the Fernie Chase. *Master Ruan* was quoted at 6–4, *Lovat* was at 2–1 and *Royal Mond* 9–4. There is no record of what odds were for no horse completing the course.

Royal Mond went down at the very first fence, and *Master Ruan* slipped on landing after clearing it, unseating jockey Freeman. *Lovat*, the only horse left with virtually the whole course in front of him, then unseated jockey Mann after jumping the water and the chase was on from there.

Master Ruan's trainer, George Archibald, spotting the state of the race, ran after the riderless horse and mounted

Master Ruan himself, riding him back to the first fence, where Freeman was waiting. The jockey remounted and set off towards the second obstacle. After two refusals, *Master Ruan* jumped it and was back in the race.

Lovat's jockey, Mann, also remounted, but the horse repeatedly refused the next fences. Various people did their best to shoo the horse on, but they were forced to give it up as a hopeless cause. That left Freeman and *Master Ruan* in charge of the race. The horse was more 'in charge' than the jockey.

After four refusals at the water jump, *Master Ruan* finally cleared the obstacle, accompanied by a small cheer from those few spectators who could afford to stay late in case the race was ever finished. But *Master Ruan*'s seven refusals at the next fence tested everybody's patience, so the judge called it a day, the race was declared void and everyone went home.

SCOTLAND YARD INVESTIGATES

BATH, JULY 1953

The gang bought two bay colts in France. *Francasal*, who had been placed only once in six outings, cost £820. The other horse, *Santa Amaro*, a £2,000 buy, showed much better form than *Francasal* when the men organised a discreet Worcester trial two months before the Spa Selling Plate at Bath.

On Sunday 12 July, both horses were shipped from France to Folkestone. On first sight, they looked similar, but an expert could tell the difference by a white spot on the withers of one horse and distinctive saddle-marks.

The transport contractor made the switch – by mistake, he claimed – and the horse called *Santa Amaro* went to an Epsom trainer, who knew the animal as *Francasal*. The real *Francasal* went to a different yard, where it was also known as *Francasal*. On Thursday 16 July, the day of the Spa Selling Plate at 2p.m., both horses left their relative stables, one bound for Newmarket, the other for Bath. Both *Santa Amaro* and *Francasal* were entered for the Spa Selling Plate and a race at Newmarket. The real *Francasal* went neither to Bath nor Newmarket but on a pointless journey to nowhere. Newmarket racecourse received a strange message to say that *Santa Amaro*'s horsebox had broken down at Stevenage and therefore the horse wouldn't run at Newmarket. This was strange because, in the days before overnight declarations, it was common for a horse to be declared a non-runner through simply failing to show. No reason was necessary.

So, to review the complicated scenario around noon on the Thursday of Bath races, *Francasal* was in the middle of nowhere going nowhere, while *Santa Amaro* was heading towards Bath under the name of Francasal.

At precisely 1.30p.m. that day, two men set about a task in Bath's Lansdown Lane. One of them, a Welsh rag and scrap-metal dealer, steadied the bottom of a double-extension ladder. The other held a blowlamp and began to climb.

'What are you doing?' asked one of the local residents, who was cutting roadside grass.

'I have a job to do,' said the man with the oxy-acetylene welding torch. He climbed the ladder and began using the blowlamp on the lead-covered telephone cable. Bath racecourse was three-quarters of a mile away.

The local resident looked closely at the brick-red 30-cwt Bedford lorry with its dropped tailboard. He noted part of the lorry's registration number.

The man with the blowlamp cut through the telephone cable and Bath racecourse was left with no lines. People supposed a severe local thunderstorm was to blame. Reporters were forced to use a shuttle taxi service to a public telephone 2 miles (3.2km) away. Bookmakers outside Bath could not telephone the course to tell of large bets being placed.

In the half-hour before the race, a bookmaking business, owned by the gang, laid off bets worth £3,580 on *Francasal* through other bookmakers. As individuals, they bet a further £2,500 on the horse. The money was spread around the country, but, because the bookmakers could not get on the blower to Bath, the horse's odds remained at 10–1.

Shortly before 2p.m., William Gilchrist received his riding instructions from the Epsom trainer. Both men presumed they were talking about a horse called *Francasal*. Gilchrist went to the front early in the race and '*Francasal*' won comfortably by 2 lengths. At the eventual auction, the conspirators bought back the horse for 740 guineas. The gang now stood to win around £60,000 from their bets.

National bookmaking organisations were suspicious. They urged their members not to pay out immediately while Scotland Yard investigations into wire-cutting were under way. Within three weeks Scotland Yard had arrested the Welsh lorry-driver seen in Lansdown Lane on the day of the race. He received a three-month sentence under section 37 of the 1861 Malicious Damage Act, but was absent from his own trial because he was already serving three months for maintenance arrears. The job at Bath paid him £35.

The prize money for the Spa Selling Plate – all £188 of it – was held back, and the Clerk of the Course at Bath lodged an objection to the winner of the 2 o'clock race, on the grounds that *Francasal* was not *Francasal*. Within six months it was clear that *Francasal*, the winner of the Spa Selling Plate, was really *Santa Amaro*. Evidence of this was built up from a number of sources – the farrier who put racing shoes on *Santa Amaro* before the Bath race, the Folkestone veterinary surgeon, the transporter, the trainers who had seen the horses and *Francasal*'s listed trainer, who had never seen the horse and who was named by the gang without his authorisation. Scotland Yard's case was helped enormously by locating the two horses at Sonning Common, near Reading – had the horses been returned to France, the criminals might have won their £60,000 – but the five men arrested could not be linked to the cutting of telephone lines in Lansdown Lane.

When the case went to court, in January 1954, five men were accused of conspiring to defraud Bath Racecourse Company. A 16-day trial ended in strange circumstances. The jury could not agree a verdict. In fact, according to the foreman, they couldn't agree *on anything*. A retrial was the outcome, 23 more days were spent in court, and four convictions were obtained. A fifth man was found 'not guilty'.

All bets on *Francasal* were eventually declared void.

A RACE FOR SEVEN NOVICES

PLUMPTON, NOVEMBER 1954

A sunny day, heavy ground, and a course stretching 2 miles and 750 yards. It was the last race of the day and conditions were not very friendly for novice steeplechasers. They were even less friendly for the poor jockeys.

There were seven runners for the Cuckfield Novices' Steeplechase. They started badly and then fell away.

Top Gem, the second favourite, fell at the first fence. That left six.

But *Top Gem* also brought down *Maid of Valence* at the first. Then there were five.

After half a mile, *Dancing Warrior* fell. With almost 2 miles still to run, there were four horses left in the race.

One of the riderless horses jumped short at the water, and this caused problems for the four remaining runners. *Greenfax*, the 5–4 favourite, *Canon Flame* and *Magna Carta* fell at the water. And then there was one, *Struell Well*, but *Magna Carta* was remounted. A two-horse race, with a circuit of Plumpton remaining.

Magna Carta refused at the next. Again there was one. *Struell Well* fell at the next, but Alan Oughton also remounted, and was able to continue what in another setting would have been one of the worst show-jumping rounds on record. *Struell Well* scrambled over the next fence, barely made it over the water, looked very shaky at the one after, then refused one and clambered over at the second attempt.

Somehow Oughton managed to coax *Struell Well* to the second fence from home, but the horse refused, dumping Oughton on the other side of the fence. *Struell Well* did his best to hide in the open ditch, but Oughton was persistent, as described by Meyrick Good in *Sporting Life*: 'Alan Oughton went round the fence, and, in order to get his horse out of the ditch, had to take him on to the centre of the course. He then remounted, and made his way through the cars to the entrance to the course by the judge's box.'

When they saw Oughton riding *Struell Well* up the public side of the rails towards the stands, most onlookers thought it signalled the end of the race. The judge left his box and was presumed to have gone for his tea, and the boards were put down on the course to enable the spectators to walk across to the car-park. Night was not far away.

But Oughton was still trying. Finally he reached where he had been before, back on the course with two fences to negotiate. The judge returned to his box, the planks were removed from the course, and there was a big cheer as Oughton and *Struell Well* – starting price 11–2 – came in to try the second from last one more time. The horse refused.

Struell Well did not look as if he was jumping any more fences that day. So, rather than ask for the key to the changing-room and promise to lock up when he had completed the course, Oughton opted to retire and lead his horse back. The race was declared void, and the horses were treated as non-runners. All that for nothing ... except a worthy place in a book on strange horse races.

A HUMAN ERROR?

RIPON, APRIL 1955

Very occasionally in the history of horse racing, a judge has made a decision which has totally baffled the watching public. Usually, though, there is a logical explanation. When the result of the first race at Ripon on Saturday 30 April was announced, people were astonished that a horse well back in the running could be given first place without any objections. The reason, they implied later, was that the judge had made a simple mistake. He had identified the horse incorrectly.

There was no photographic finish at Ripon in those days, and the judge had to rely on close observation. It was always toughest in tight races, and the 2.30 5-furlong Trial Selling Plate had distances of a short head, a short head, a neck, half a length and half a length. No one disagreed with the judge on the distance verdict. No one doubted that the judge had a difficult decision in such a tight race.

Three horses reached the line in a bunch. *Singaria*, correctly placed second by the judge, and *Merry Pat*, rightly placed third, were on the outside of this bunch of three. Most onlookers thought the horse in the middle was *Golden Decree*, a 25–1 shot owned by Lord Decies. The trainer of *Golden Decree*, Colonel Lyde, was confident that the filly had been placed. However, this horse was ignored in the placings, whereas *Blue Comet*, the 7–2 favourite, was announced as the winner.

'A. Roberts appeared to be ready to dismount *Blue Comet* on returning to the paddock until his attention was drawn to the number board,' documented *Sporting Life*, 'after which he rode H. Barker's charge into the winner's enclosure.'

Blue Comet, owned by Mrs G.W. Ferguson and trained by Barker, was recorded for posterity as the winner. But many believed that the judge had simply identified the horse incorrectly. *Golden Decree*'s jockey wore royal blue and yellow quarters and a blue cap. *Blue Comet* carried colours of royal blue and light blue quarters, with a blue cap which had a yellow hoop. Had the favourite been ousted in favour of a 25–1 outsider, then we might have heard more of it. As it was, no objection was lodged.

In recent times, the Jockey Club has looked closely at the use of colour photographs of close finishes, and this is now possible, although the development time is a little longer than for black and white. Confusing colours might happen only once a generation, but officials recognise that it is worth preventing. However, there is nothing one can do if a judge makes a mistake or if it is not possible to use camera equipment. An instance of the first was a race at Thirsk in 1911, when everybody could see that *Formamint* beat *Ask Papa* by about 2 lengths, but the judge decided Ask Papa had won by half a length. And an instance of the second was at Kempton Park in May 1984, when the camera operators were taking industrial action and the judge, having to learn an old skill, gave two disputed winners.

A STORM OVER ASCOT

ASCOT, JULY 1955

In retrospect, the description of Ascot in that week's *Wokingham and Bracknell Times* was exceedingly premature and tactless: 'It was a once-in-a-lifetime Ascot this week. Ascot as it should be, but seldom is, with the sun blazing from a cloudless sky and the mercury standing at a steady 80 degrees.'

Premature and tactless because, on the Thursday afternoon, presumably shortly after the newspaper had gone to press, the weather changed with dramatic and tragic effect.

Rain started about the time of the 3.45 race, the Gold Vase, won by *Prince Barle* at 11–2. The crowd rushed towards the covered areas and huddled inside the tea-tent and under the ice-cream stand. 'A number of men in the Royal enclosure lost their hats in the rush for shelter,' commented *The Times*. And a number of women, inappropriately dressed in short-sleeve summer frocks, were quick off the mark too. Other women, despite the heat, had opted to parade coats and stoles of mink, ocelot and sable anyway.

Next, thunder roared through the sky.

In the densely packed crowd at the centre of the course, opposite the royal enclosure, a child was passed over people's heads towards a safer area at the rear.

Then came the lightning.

There were three flashes within a second or two. They

appeared to strike a metal fence near where the bulk of the crowd were sheltering. People fell to the ground, and witnesses later used phrases like 'as if mown down', 'toppled like dominoes' and 'like a pack of cards'.

Many of the crowd suffered a moment's black-out. Then they heard the screaming and saw the panic of people apprehensive of more lightning flashes. The police restored calm, and Windsor Hospital went on alert.

Two people died and 42 others were injured, 18 of them detained at Windsor Hospital. The two who died were the wife of an electrical engineer from Reading, pregnant with their first child, and a Sheffield man who was an evangelist with the London Open Air Mission.

The next race on the Ascot card, the 4.20 Ribblesdale Stakes, was delayed until 5.05 but still went ahead. The last two races, the 4.55 and the 5.30, were not surprisingly postponed.

DEVON LOCH AT AINTREE
AINTREE, LIVERPOOL, MARCH 1956

'The calamity which overtook us was sudden, terrible and completely without warning to either the horse or me. In one stride he was bounding smoothly along, a poem of controlled motion; in the next his hind legs stiffened and refused to function.'

The story of the calamity of *Devon Loch*, the horse that collapsed 50 yards (45.7m) from winning the 1956 Grand National, really belongs to Dick Francis. Francis experienced it, resolved it and wrote it, as quoted above. But a book on strange horse races must include a terse reference to one of the most dramatic mood-swinging incidents in the history of the sport.

Devon Loch, owned by the Queen Mother, was an Irish-bred horse trained by Peter Cazalet and ridden by Dick Francis in some of his earlier races. Francis had always fancied the horse, and a cracked collar-bone, received 15 days before the Grand National, was not enough to put the jockey off what promised to be an exciting, optimistic ride. The reality broke the limits of expectation. Except for a near mishap two fences after Valentine's on the first circuit, when *Devon Loch* changed direction in mid-air to avoid the fallen *Domata*, the horse gave Francis a dream ride.

Devon Loch came to the front with three fences to jump. At each jump the horse pulled further and further away, sailing over the fences as though they were hurdles. He met the last fence a length and a half clear of *ESB* and pulled away on landing. It looked like the first Royal Grand National winner for 56 years and a first-ever Grand National winner for trainer Peter Cazalet, who had known disappointment when *Davy Jones* ran out after a buckle of the reins came apart near the finish of the 1936 Grand National, and again in the 1948 Grand National when Lord Mildmay would probably have won had he not suffered neck trouble during the race.

'In all my life I have never experienced a greater joy than the knowledge that I was going to win the National,' wrote Francis in *Sport of Queens*, the autobiography which examines the *Devon Loch* finish.

The horse was fresh, the rhythm was good, and *Devon Loch* was still drawing away. The crowd cheered. How the crowd cheered. They cheered for the Queen Mother, they cheered for the Royal party, they cheered for Dick Francis and those who had backed *Devon Loch* at 100–7 cheered for themselves.

Then came the calamity. Fifty yards from the finish, the horse's ears pricked, he raised his fore legs as if to take off and jump, then fell flat on his belly and splayed his legs out sideways and backwards. When *Devon Loch* stood up, he could hardly move. *ESB*, ridden by Dave Dick, went past to win the 1956 Grand National.

In his autobiography, Francis looks closely at the possible reasons for the strange behaviour of the horse. He discounts the 'heart attack' theory, as the horse was fine immediately before and after the incident, and, anyway, Francis had experience of horses with heart trouble and they didn't behave like *Devon Loch*. He dismisses the 'ghost-jump' theory that *Devon Loch* was trying to leap the water-jump (on the other side of the rails) on the grounds that it is an insult to the horse's intelligence. He more ponderously eliminates the theory of sudden cramp because it doesn't explain why the horse pricked up his ears immediately before the belly-flop, although Francis admits that his own immediate reaction had been to think the horse had broken a hind leg.

The most logical explanation, Francis thought, was the uniqueness of the moment – the loud crescendo of cheering, a new experience for the horse, perhaps unsurpassed at Aintree. Close to the finishing-post, equine adrenalin fired up, *Devon Loch*'s intelligence and sensitivity were working so well that a puzzling, frightening, novel sound carried to his ears. Years later, even *Red Rum* was moved by a rapturous welcome.

Devon Loch's fears were over in a moment, probably because the cheering stopped as soon as he fell. The crowd's mood turned to anguish, disbelief and anti-climax, all except those who had followed *ESB* with favour. The discussion would continue, and Dick Francis, as an indirect consequence of the strange race, would embark on his second career, that of a writer.

AN ANNOUNCEMENT TO FOLLOW

WARWICK, FEBRUARY 1958

On the first circuit of the Gaydon Hunters' Steeplechase, the 2.30 race at Warwick on 1 February, *Poor Tips* fell at the second fence. The unfortunate horse – poor *Poor Tips* – was fatally injured and the course staff could not move her before the horses were approaching again.

As the horses came round on the second circuit, *Poor Tips* was out of sight on the far side of the fence. An ambulance man, thinking quickly, flagged the jockeys and diverted the whole field round the fence. So all the horses left in the race missed jumping that fence on the second circuit.

The first horse past the finishing-post was a 15-year-old hunter called *Airmail IV*, ridden by Mr J. Thorne. A clear two lengths separated *Airmail IV* from the second horse, *Jockey Blue*, with *Song of India* back in third. There seemed no possible doubt about the order of the horses, and no need to consult the photo-finish equipment. The announcement over the loudspeaker was therefore strange: 'The result of this race will be announced in a few minutes.'

In fact it took 12 days.

The local stewards, reacting quickly on the day of the race, allowed the result to stand. A later inquiry, however, found that they had no option under the provisions of rule 134 (4) but to declare the race void. This decision was announced in the *Racing Calendar*, but some bets had already been paid out on the 'winning' *Airmail IV*.

Some years later, in March 1987, there was a similar incident at Stratford. When five horses came round to jump the last open ditch on the third circuit of the EBF Novices' Chase, two jockeys lay injured on the landing side. Carroll Gray had fallen first time round, Mark Hoad on the second circuit, and both were not to be moved. Simon Sherwood and Mark Perrett, jockeys already out of the race, took the sensible precaution of standing 20 yards (18.3m) apart in front of the fence and diverting the remaining horses round it. Yet the race was declared void.

TROUBLE ON THE TRACK
DURBAN, SOUTH AFRICA,
DECEMBER 1958

Where there is money, there will be crime chasing it, and horse racing has historically been burdened with fraud and sporadic outbursts of violence. What has worried officials more in recent years is whether horse racing might replace soccer as a setting for a subculture of aggression. There are plenty of examples of race meetings becoming strange through a backcloth of violence, but only occasionally, as in this case, does the crowd attack the horses and jockeys while a race is in progress.

The Clairwood Turf Club were staging their Christmas meeting, and there was plenty of good cheer on Boxing Day ... until the eighth race. Twenty-three horses lined up and the starter pulled the handle. For a moment the start looked a good one, but then *Oleate* swerved in front of *Meadow View* and *Certain Saint*, two fancied horses, and put them out of the race. *Molly Mallory* whipped round and refused to start.

On a day when the first seven races had included five short-priced winners, the crowd were very hopeful of *Meadow View* (at 6–4) and *Certain Saint*. Now many were left with no interest in the race. They were furious and expected the race to be rerun. It wasn't. The start was held to be good.

Under the apartheid system, there were two enclosures at the Clairwood course – one for whites and one for non-whites – but the spectators reacted as one, all demanding that the race be rerun or bets refunded. The stewards announced an inquiry into the start of the race, but that wasn't enough to pacify the angry spectators who were demonstrating on the course when the ninth race was about to start.

They were given five minutes to clear the track, and the police ushered them to the 'appropriate' enclosure. The ninth race started. In retrospect, it was a mistake.

As the horses passed the 3-furlong mark, they were attacked by the crowd. Spectators ripped out pieces of fencing and threw palings on to the course. They hurled stones at the horses and jockeys. A mob surged across the track in front of the horses. They threw bottles and other missiles from very close range. They were so near to their targets that one spectator was knocked over by a horse. Women screamed. Some spectators turned away, not bearing to watch as the horses toppled over and jockeys lay injured on the track. A few horses swerved through the crowd and made it to the finishing-post.

The drama wasn't over. Police reinforcements arrived to disperse the crowd, but a group of whites later stoned the horses again when they were being loaded into railway vehicles ready to leave town.

Two horses ambushed on the track, Mr R.S. Whiteford's *Joyously* and Mrs J.H. Venter's *Lady Love*, were destroyed after their injuries had been examined. *Joyously*, winner of five races, had a broken knee. *Lady Love*, winner of four races, had a fractured shoulder. Another horse, Mr J. Angles' *Finisterre*, had a broken bone in the nose, a chest wound and an injured knee, and other horses suffered cuts and bruises.

Five jockeys needed hospital treatment. Three of them, Cyril Buckham (broken nose and other injuries), Percy Cayeux (concussion) and A. Miller (bruises), were fit within a few days, but Terry Doo, whose left arm was injured by a paling, was out of racing for a couple of weeks. The fifth, Basil Lewis, a leading South African jockey, was fortunate not to lose an eye. Wearing goggles saved his left eye from being gouged out, but he needed a facial operation. He was back in action within a week.

SEVEN FALL IN THE DERBY

EPSOM DOWNS, JUNE 1962

There were 26 runners in the 1962 Derby Stakes, and they got away at 3.27, seven minutes after the scheduled time. *Romancero* went into a 3-length lead and kept it until nearing Tattenham Corner. Six furlongs from home, where the course went downhill and bent to the left in preparation for Tattenham Corner, the pile-up occurred.

With hindsight, it was obvious that horses at the front, like *Romancero*, were falling back at this stage of the race, whereas horses at the back, like the favourite *Heathersett*, were picking up pace and closing as a bunch. In addition, as the horses were perhaps seven or eight abreast, jockeys on the outside were edging towards the rails, looking for a shorter way home.

The result was a crowded collision.

No jockey was to blame, the Epsom stewards said later, and it was difficult to spot the order of events. Probably *Romulus* and *Crossen* fell first, after either striking the heels of the horses in front or hitting each other. After that, five more horses tumbled dangerously – *Changing Times*, *Persian Fancy*, *King Canute II*, *Pindaric* and *Heathersett*. *Spartan General* jumped over two fallers, and *Larkspur*'s jockey Neville Sellwood lost ground but did well to avoid the fallers. Four or five other horses were interfered with by the incident.

The remainder of the field careered down the home stretch chased by six riderless horses. (*King Canute II* was humanely destroyed.) *Valentine* had the lead coming out of Tattenham Corner, then *Escort* and then *River Chanter*, who was looking fairly strong. But Sellwood was still going very well on *Larkspur*. Two furlongs from home, *Larkspur* took up the running and went on to win comfortably. *Arcor* came with a late run to pip *Le Cantilien* for second place, giving French horses second and third.

The casualty list was another matter. Harry Carr was badly concussed, Wally Swinburn had a neck injury, Stan Smith had concussion and a broken leg, Tommy Gosling was kept in hospital overnight with concussion, and Laurraun and Lewis were treated for arm and hand injuries. R.P. Elliott was the only jockey to walk away relatively unscathed. Three fallen horses were badly cut, but only the unfortunate *King Canute II* was not fit enough to chase the pack.

It was the first Derby success for both Vincent O'Brien, *Larkspur*'s trainer, and the Australian jockey Neville Sellwood. Sired by *Never Say Die*, winner of the Derby and St Leger in 1954, *Larkspur* was owned by Raymond Guest, an American from Virginia. At 22–1 he had proved a good winner, even allowing for the tragedy near Tattenham Corner.

The Epsom stewards studied two amateur films made of the incident, then absolved jockeys of blame and stated that there was no evidence of any rough riding. However, they did issue words of caution to the owners and trainers. They regretted 'that so many horses which had no right to be in the field were allowed by owners and trainers to start'. The combination of poor horses falling back, good horses moving up and badly placed horses switching inside was too much for safety.

PIONEERING A NEW COURSE

CHELTENHAM, DECEMBER 1964

Whereas horses like *Devon Loch* were never able to inform us what they were thinking and feeling when they threw away a race they had virtually won, the more articulate jockeys can reveal a lot when they are seen to behave strangely with a race all but won. In the Whaddon Amateur Riders' Handicap Chase on Saturday 12 December, John Lawrence (later Lord Oaksey) made an unusual, yet understandable error to turn a straightforward race into a strange one.

The seven runners were quickly whittled down to two. *Pay Pol*, the 9–4 favourite, fell at the sixth, bringing down *Wilmslow Boy*. *Celadon* fell at the seventh and brought down *Kingston-By-Pass*. *Captain Hornblower* went at the ninth but was trailing badly anyway. That left *Pioneer Spirit*, ridden by John Lawrence, jumping well and in total control of the race, and *French Cottage*.

When Lawrence took his mount over the second last, he was 30 lengths in front of Bill Tellwright on *French Cottage*, the only other horse in the race. *Pioneer Spirit* moved on towards the last hurdle, and the race – over a distance of 3 miles, 1 furlong and a few yards – was virtually decided.

Then Lawrence did something strange. He pulled his horse to a stop.

This was quite an achievement in itself, because the horse was going so well. So why did he do it?

The jockey believed he had taken the wrong course. It was

early in the day, not yet 1 o'clock, and there had been some changes in the Cheltenham course. On jumping the second last, the future peer found he couldn't see the final fence. All he could see was a flight of hurdles, so he looked for an exit that would enable him to reach the fence. Of course, there was no exit. He was on the correct course, and the rails would have guided him round to the last fence on the steeplechase course if he had stayed with them.

'There was no excuse for the error,' commented the *Sporting Life*, 'but with so many courses here nowadays, the place looks more like Clapham Junction than a racecourse.'

Bill Tellwright swept past on *French Cottage* to win by a distance at 10–1. As *Pioneer Spirit* was well-backed at 11–4, the horse's jockey did not qualify for a champagne reception. In fact, Lord Oaksey, recalling the tale for the benefit of Brough Scott's readers in the *Sunday Times* (17 January 1988), pointed out that he was booed by the crowd, was nursing a back injury from the action of pulling the horse up so suddenly, and, when he arrived home and ran the water for a bath, was interrupted by a telephone call such that water overflowed and the ceiling fell into the dining room. Not a great day for him.

A MILLION TO ONE

HALDON, DEVON, SEPTEMBER 1965

It is a sad feature of horse racing that there are casualties – humans and horses – but what odds would a bookmaker give on two horses dying from heart attacks in a seven-horse race?

The 3p.m. race at the Devon and Exeter course on 1 September was the Seaton Selling Handicap. It was run over 2 miles, and the clear favourite, *Galatea* at 8–11, had the race sewn up approaching the last hurdle. Ten lengths clear, *Galatea* suddenly failed to rise to the last, put jockey Paul Cook and herself on the floor and interfered with the rest of the field.

Jungle Student, ridden by John Haine, came through to win as a 20–1 outsider. *Will Rogers* (100–30) took second place, and *Quel Diable* (8–1) was third. What happened next was later described as a million-to-one chance.

Jungle Student, a seven-year-old bay gelding by *Kings Scholarship* and *Jungle Treasure*, collapsed a few yards past the winning-post and died of heart failure. *Galatea*, the fallen favourite, a nine-year-old mare, struggled to her feet, passed the post riderless and collapsed and died, also of heart failure, close to where *Jungle Student* lay. The £186 prize money was still presented to Mrs E.M. Aldis, owner of *Jungle Student*. The horse was trained by A. Gilbert, who had recently moved from Andoversford near Cheltenham to Newcastle Emlyn in Dyfed (then in Cardiganshire).

Galatea, the only horse in the race to fall, was owned by Mr W.H. Tosh, and the horse had won over the same course earlier in the season. She was trained by L. Kennard at Broadhembury.

After the two deaths, the day held a few more incidents.

The next race, the St David's three-year-old hurdle race, was won by *Acrovat*, but *Eversley*, a horse trained by Fred Rimell, broke a fetlock and had to be destroyed. And the race after that brought a dead heat between *Vindicated* and *Streamer*.

'MAN WITH GUN HOLDS UP RACE'

FLEMINGTON, MELBOURNE, FEBRUARY 1966

Walter Hoysted was a frustrated man. He believed fervently that whipping a racehorse was the worst form of cruelty, especially when a horse was doing all it could to win a race, but his campaign to stop whipping had not yet worked. He had written to newspapers, written to the Commissioner of Police, written to Victoria Racing Club members and even written to the Chief Secretary. Little had happened, apart from a few interesting editorials. It was time for more drastic action.

Hoysted wrote again to the Victoria Racing Club to say that if they didn't take drastic action by Saturday 19 February, the start of the next race meeting, then he would.

So he did.

As the runners went to the start for the 2-mile Fulham Hurdle, the first race of the meeting, Walter Hoysted appeared in front of the starting-stalls carrying a double-barrelled shotgun in his right hand and a box of cartridges in his left. He fired a shotgun blast into the air and warned everyone to stand clear.

The jockeys were told by officials to keep away from the starting-stalls. They circled their horses about a furlong from the start, and officials and police tried to deal with Walter Hoysted.

Hoysted was known to the track. He had once been a professional jockey for five years, but weight problems had driven him out of the sport after some success. Now 52 years old, he worked as a driver.

Police Constable Berry crept to within four feet of Hoysted.

The former jockey swivelled round and pointed the gun directly at the policeman.

'Don't come any closer,' Hoysted said. 'I'm fair dinkum. Don't try to make a hero out of yourself.'

Constable Berry kept back. Only Hoysted knew that the safety-catch was on the gun.

Hoysted made more announcements to the 20 or so people in the vicinity: 'It's a nice state of affairs when a man has to make a fool of himself to get justice.'

'If you don't surrender your gun, we'll call your father to the track,' said the course manager, and this tactic worked. Hoysted gave up the shotgun and the policeman took him away to press charges.

The Fulham Hurdle started 16 minutes late. It was won by *With Discretion*. Why is it that so many horses seem aptly named?

The local newspapers reported the event – 'Man with gun holds up race' said one headline – and, nine days later, Walter Hoysted was fined a total of $80 (£32) on three charges. He was found guilty of unlawfully assaulting PC Berry, being armed with an offensive weapon and firing without permission.

'Someone had to do this,' he told the court. 'Someone had to force the whole matter into a court.'

'Mr Hoysted is perhaps a humanist ten years ahead of his time,' said Frank Galbally, his solicitor.

NINE OUT OF TEN DISQUALIFIED

MARKET RASEN, MARCH 1966

The 2p.m. race at Market Rasen was the Cox Moore Sweaters Handicap Steeplechase, with most of the £758 prize money being raised by the proprietors of the sweater firm at Long Eaton. There were ten runners, and nine were disqualified. According to the *Market Rasen Mail*, it was 'a spectacle without precedent in local racing history'.

The trouble came at the tenth fence, which was divided to make two obstacles – an open ditch on the stands side and a plain fence on the other. The horses, following each other like sheep, jumped the open ditch on the stands side. All except one. John Buckingham, on Edward Courage's *Lira*, felt certain that the plain fence was the correct one for the second circuit, so he moved the horse across and jumped that one instead. Most of the 6,000 spectators assumed that *Lira* had made the mistake.

John Buckingham, now a jockeys' valet, recalls the knowledge that went into his decision that day: 'I knew that course well and had ridden there a lot. I'd even ridden it before with *Lira*, the mare I was riding that day. The fence in question, either the second or the third, could be either a ditch or a fence. We went three times round the course, and when we came to this fence on the second circuit I could see they'd moved the flag over so I shouted to one or two of the jockeys that they were going the wrong way. Another thing that convinced me was that in a 3-mile chase in those days you only jumped three ditches. We'd jumped the ditch on this fence on the first circuit and we'd jumped one round the back that we were going to jump again so that made three. I was adamant I was right, even when the other jockeys tried to get me to pull up at every fence after that!'

George Lee took *Hyanna* past the finishing-post first, thinking he had notched up his first winner of the season. Buckingham's *Lira* finished second, two lengths away, the jockey not pushing her too hard because he knew he would either win the race or be disqualified, and *Dorenco* came in a poor third, 15 lengths adrift. As soon as the last horse had passed the finishing-post, a stewards' inquiry was announced. Buckingham chipped in with his own objection to the winner.

The stewards soon satisfied themselves that the course was correctly dolled off and flagged off, and nine horses had in fact jumped the wrong tenth fence. As Mr V.J. Lucas, the race executive, pointed out, everything was just as it had been for a 3-mile race for 20 years, and all had run smoothly in the past. It should have been quite clear which was the correct course, but perhaps a jockey new to the course had led the others down the wrong path.

Nine horses were disqualified, and Buckingham, the only finisher, won the race for Edward Courage. And that after Mrs Courage had told him off for going the wrong way.

A SHOT HORSE

DURBAN, SOUTH AFRICA, JULY 1966

At 6.15a.m. on 10 June, a wintry morning in Durban, a well-dressed man of European origins hid in a concrete shelter at the southern end of the Rupert Ellis Viaduct. He was there to earn 10,000 rand (£5,000). In the holster under his arm he carried a pistol with a barrel 1½in (3.8cm) long. Inside the barrel was a soft-nosed lead cartridge. The man took out his pistol and waited.

The string of horses trained by Syd Laird approached the concrete shelter as they headed for their morning exercise on Blue Lagoon Beach. They included *Sea Cottage*, a legend in South Africa and the clear favourite for the Durban July Handicap and the Clairwood Winter Handicap, two of the biggest races of the year, the first less than a month away.

Although physically unattractive, *Sea Cottage* was entirely lovable. He won virtually all his races by producing a late, electrifying burst of long-striding speed to come from the back and burn off the opposition with ease. In the string this morning he held a nondescript position, towards the rear, but was easily identifiable. He was the horse with a distinctive white blaze and white hoof markings, the only one tended by *two* grooms.

The man in the concrete shelter recognised the horse and pointed his pistol. From a range of 20ft (6.1m), he shot *Sea Cottage*. The horse reared as the bullet hit his hind leg, and the other animals were startled by the noise. Amid the chaos which followed, only the most observant of people could have noticed the gunman run for his car, jump in and roar off. But someone did notice.

The man was arrested and two other men were incriminated. The pre-trial alleged that a local bookmaker stood to lose so much from a *Sea Cottage* victory in the July Handicap that he had arranged the shooting, using an intermediary to hire the gunman, who was a gambling club manager. After examining the bookmaker's books, the state opted not to prosecute the bookmaker for his role in the shooting, preferring to bring a charge of fraud which resulted in a verdict of 'not guilty'. But the gunman was sentenced to six years' imprisonment.

After the shooting, *Sea Cottage* walked home, went lame, and was treated for shock, pain and bruising. The bullet was assumed to be lost inside the horse, which added to the legend. Arguments broke out as to whether bets on *Sea Cottage* for the July Handicap should be valid. The horse was initially assumed to be a likely non-runner but, after treatment with enzymes and butazolidin, plus infra-red and ultra-sonic treatment, the horse recovered amazingly. He ran in the July Handicap and came fourth.

Two weeks later, as 4–7 favourite for the Clairwood Winter Handicap, *Sea Cottage* lay almost last as the horses came into the straight. Robert Sivewright rode him wide on the outside and the horse achieved what seemed almost impossible to win by half a length.

The following year *Sea Cottage* dead-heated for first place with *Jollify* in the July Handicap, and the people's equine hero eventually ended his career with 20 wins out of 24.

NO COW, NO JOCKEYS
ACCRA, GHANA, AUGUST 1966

The trouble escalated on Thursday 18 August, the second day of the two-week race meeting at the Accra Turf Club. The jockeys invited senior officials of the Turf Club to a meeting, and stated their case. They thought it was time for a cow on the racetrack.

The jockeys were very worried by the dangers of a bend at the 6-furlong mark on the Accra course. The bend had been the scene of 11 recent accidents, taking the lives of two jockeys and two horses. Naturally, the jockeys wanted some action to be taken. What they suggested was the purchase of a sacrificial cow, which could be slaughtered at the 6-furlong mark in order to purify the corner and prevent further bad fortune. As a sign of their intent, the jockeys showed that they had collected 96 cedis (about £40) towards the cost of the cow. They hoped the Accra Turf Club would contribute the rest. The threat of a boycott was mentioned by the jockeys.

Mr C.W. Quist, acting chairman of the Turf Club, was not very hopeful. He pointed out that a cow hardly constituted 'ordinary recurrent expenditure' and therefore he couldn't allocate funds until the next stewards' meeting – a week later. Quist was asked to attend a larger meeting of jockeys the next day, because the jockeys' representatives didn't think the story would be believed by his colleagues. A week seemed too long to wait.

The jockeys met the next day without Turf Club officials. They were disappointed that no sacrificial cow was being made available immediately and disgusted with the behaviour of the Turf Club officials. The majority of the jockeys voted to boycott the next day of the meeting, the Saturday.

On Saturday 20 August there was pandemonium at the racetrack. Fifty-five licensed jockeys joined the boycott, and only 11 jockeys were not affected. The first race was delayed for an hour while Turf Club officials tried to persuade jockeys and apprentice jockeys at the racetrack to ride. Eventually, enough jockeys were found to make a race of it, and *Too Far* came home in front of *Hankuri* and *Marone* to win over 8 furlongs.

When the Turf Club stewards did meet, in the middle of the following week, they were discussing the boycott rather than expenditure for a sacrificial cow. The 55 licensed jockeys involved were banned for the rest of the meeting (until 3 September) and fined 60 cedis (about £25) each. They couldn't enter the racecourse without the stewards' permission. The banned jockeys included top names in Ghana like Kantara Kamara, Isa Allassan, Amadu Allassan and Seidu Alash, but the champion jockey, Mahdi, was still riding. The apprentice jockeys, on the other hand, were each fined only 30 cedis and they were free to ride.

The race meeting continued to its end, with many an apprentice being given an unexpected start to his career.

THIRTY-SIX HORSES DIE AFTER RACE

DE AAR, SOUTH AFRICA, OCTOBER 1966

Nearly 100 horses took part in the annual 100-mile (161km) marathon horse race across the arid countryside of Northern Cape Province, and, within a week of completing the 50-mile (80.5km) first leg, 36 horses were dead. Needless to say, the second 50-mile leg was cancelled.

The 50-mile ride took place on Friday 7 October. By 7p.m. that evening, the first ten horses had died. The initial conclusion was that the horses were dying from heart disease, and local police did not suspect foul play. People were talking about the exceptionally hot weather for October, though it was not as hot as it could get in December. On the other hand, the previous year's marathon had a longer first leg than 50 miles, and only one horse, destroyed after breaking a leg, had died that year.

As the deaths increased, suspicions were alerted. On the Monday, the number of deaths was up to 33, and a senior CID official from Kimberley was called in to investigate. Nitrate poisoning was suspected now, and one theory suggested that someone had visited the De Aar stadium on Thursday night and sprinkled poison into the horses' fodder.

But why would anyone do it?

It seemed unlikely that animal-lovers would poison so many horses in order to have a race banned because they thought it was cruel to horses, unless a plan had backfired and the poison had been stronger than expected. Nor did it seem likely that a contestant would poison so many rival horses to improve the chances of winning a prize worth only 500 rand.

On the assumption of nitrate poisoning – safe at 20 grammes, poisonous at 50 grammes – the ill horses were treated with methylene blue, injected in two-gramme quantities. The eventual death toll, though, rose to 36 horses. They were buried in a mass grave outside De Aar, and their value was put at about 10,000 rand.

Major C.A. Cloete, in charge of the case, authorised samples to be sent away for analysis. The results were surprising. All tests were negative. The official report indicated that the horses died from acetonuria.

On 26 October, the state veterinarian at De Aar, Dr E.M. van Tonder, announced that he would conduct his own investigation into the deaths. Unlike the police analysts, he had seen the horses while they were still alive but ill. He was familiar with acetonuria, but still suspected some form of poisoning.

The police, as they say, had nothing to go on.

FOINAVON'S NATIONAL
AINTREE, LIVERPOOL, APRIL 1967

It was an eventful Grand National that year, even before the race began: eleven days before the race, vandals damaged the rebuilt Canal Turn fence, shattered windows in the stand, and ripped out washbasins and toilet-bowls, so dogs were brought in to guard the course; the favourite, *Highland Wedding*, who would win in 1969, withdrew through injury; a 67-year-old American owner-rider called Tim Durant negotiated odds of 15–1 with Ladbrokes that he would complete the Aintree course on *Aerial III*; there were the perennial discussions about whether this was the last Grand National or not in the light of uncertainty about the Topham ownership of the course; and arrangements were made to televise the race across the Atlantic for the first time.

What must first-time viewers have thought of the 1967 Grand National, one of the oddest in the event's history?

Forty-four runners tackled the course, and they progressed with no more than the usual quota of mishaps until they reached the 23rd fence, ironically the smallest fence on the course. There was a still a big field, and much of the really hard work was done, Becher's Brook left behind for the second time. Then a loose horse called *Popham Down* precipitated one of the biggest shambles a racecourse has ever seen.

Popham Down cut across the front of the fence. The two leaders stopped, and every horse in the race felt the knock-on effects. It was like a motorway accident in the fog. A real pile-up.

Stan Mellor, knocked off *The Fossa*, landed on top of the fence. John Lawrence (later Lord Oaksey) was thrown over the fence by his horse. Mellor and Lawrence ran towards the rails for safety, expecting the other horses to be powering over them. None came. Not immediately.

Horses and jockeys littered the ground at the front of the fence, and those still in partnership, like the 15–2 favourite *Honey End* and Josh Gifford, were facing the wrong way. Then came *Foinavon* and 27-year-old jockey John Buckingham.

Buckingham, who had never ridden in the Grand National before, had been offered the ride on the Wednesday before the race. He had stayed at a friend's house in Liverpool on the Friday night, sleeping uncomfortably on two armchairs pushed together. *Foinavon*, a half-brother to *Team Spirit*, bred in Ireland and named after a Scottish hill, attracted media interest mainly through having a stable companion, a white goat called Susie. There was no real racing interest in a horse quoted at 100–1. As Charles Benson of the *Daily Express* wrote on the morning of the race: '*Foinavon* has no chance. Not the boldest of jumpers, he can safely be ignored, even in a race noted for shocks.'

John Buckingham was along for the ride, surprised at how fast the other horses had gone on the first circuit. His horse had won once in 22 starts, and that was in the 1964–5 season. In the Cheltenham Gold Cup, the horse had finished a distant last, and neither the owner, Cyril Watkins, nor the trainer, John Kempton, had come to Aintree to see him perform in the Grand National. Watkins and his wife watched on television, able to spot *Foinavon* among the leaders at the first fence but resigned to the horse being out-of-camera for the rest of the race ... until the 23rd fence.

At the 23rd, John Buckingham had the peculiar advantage of being about 30 lengths behind the leaders. In front of him he saw pandemonium and a wall of horses, some fallen, some facing him. Buckingham, with extra time to assess the situation, spotted a gap, steered *Foinavon* wide to the outside and took the horse over the fence at an awkward angle of 45 degrees. *Foinavon* was the only horse in the race to clear the smallest fence on the course at the first attempt.

John Buckingham looked around. He could see no horse in front of him, no horse behind. Only then did he realise that he was in the lead.

Back at the 23rd fence, some jockeys were doing their utmost to get back into the race. *Red Alligator*, brought down, was remounted. *Honey End*, turned round by Josh Gifford, jumped the fence at the second attempt. *What a Myth* also took two attempts, but *Kapeno* needed three attempts and *Freddie* four. *Kirtle-Lad* set off in pursuit but refused the 24th fence. *Greek Scholar* was also back in the race.

Foinavon had a lead of almost two fences, but the horse was tiring and needed a lot of work. *Honey End* began to make ground – Josh Gifford brought the favourite well back into contention – but *Foinavon* plodded on to win by 15 lengths.

The 67-year-old Durant, incidentally, fell on *Aerial III*, but, the following year, on *Highlandie*, he remounted to finish 15th of 17 finishers, winning a similar bet with Ladbrokes.

Foinavon became an instant household name. Some experts were disappointed that the Grand National had been relegated to the status of farce, but others enjoyed the unpredictability of a 100–1 outsider winning the race in such bizarre circumstances. The 23rd (and seventh) fence on the Grand National course has since been renamed after *Foinavon*, who won another strange race later in his career. John Buckingham remembers riding him that day: 'It was at Uttoxeter and *Foinavon* was last of four when we came to the first in the straight. One horse fell, so I resigned myself to third place. Then another ran out and took the other one with him. I jumped the last fences on my own and the crowd went bonkers. It was the National all over again.'

NO FINISHERS IN A FLAT RACE

MARSI, MALTA, FEBRUARY 1969

The events of the third race of the fourth Winter Meeting at the Marsi racetrack were described by the *Times of Malta* as 'probably unprecedented all over the world'.

The Second-class Handicap, which was a short sprint with no obstacles, had three runners. *Plaster Saint* was ridden by J. Clifton, *Malus* had S. Sanges in the saddle, and C. D'Amato was on *Tetchy*. They started normally enough, the three runners close together at a reasonable pace. But when they reached the home stretch, the pace slowed dramatically. Were they really three horses, or were they three snails?

Tetchy's jockey slowed down so much that he stopped altogether and dismounted. About 20 yards (18.3m) further on, Sanges feigned a mishap and followed suit on *Malus*, bringing the horse to a stop and dismounting. This left *Plaster Saint* on his own, the race to himself, the other two horses completely out of the running ... if 'running' was ever the right word.

Clifton inched *Plaster Saint* towards the finishing-line. Only another 10 yards (9.1m) to go. Then, astonishingly, Clifton turned the horse away from the finishing-line and dismounted himself. Clifton and Sanges led their horses over the finishing-line by the bridles, and almost immediately there was a loudspeaker announcement – barely audible over the loud booing from the crowd – to the effect that the three jockeys and three owners were being 'warned off' indefinitely.

The jockeys' licences were withdrawn, and Sanges, also a trainer, had his trainer's licence withdrawn. The race was declared 'no race' and the betters' money was returned. Spectators wandered around the paddock, shaking their heads and mumbling words like 'deplorable' and 'disgraceful'. Two explanations were put forward: either the owners had instructed the jockeys to hold back to avoid extra handicaps, or the owners had all bet on other horses in the race. Either way, it seemed a strange way to go about it.

The next Sunday, the Marsi racetrack programme had one small change in it. The third race, the Second-class Handicap, was replaced by a 'Go as You Please' race for ponies of 13.1 hands and under, jockeys to ride in sulkies (two-wheeled carriages). Racetrack officials obviously believed that that would guarantee a better race.

RACECOURSE DOGS

REDCAR, JULY 1969

It's time for a few more equine-canine tales.

In 1837, two years after the *Queen of Trumps* episode at Doncaster, no less a race than the St Leger Stakes was affected by a dog. *Henriade*, ridden by John Day, was brought down after a collision with a stray greyhound. The dog interfered with other horses in the race.

Much more recently, there have been moments of danger and unpredictability caused by dogs joining in races. A Kelso race was run with a greyhound pacing the horses, clearing the obstacles alongside the leaders. In 1964 a black cocker spaniel did its best to lose the St Leger for Jimmy Lindley and *Indiana* in an incident not dissimilar to that affecting *Queen of Trumps* almost 130 years previously. And another St Leger, the 1948 race, saw Doug Smith helping his mount *Alycidon* to jump over a dog which ran on to the course. *Alycidon* finished second to *Black Tarquin*. In the 1926 Derby, Tommy Weston, on *Colorado*, was put off by the appearance of a dog.

At Chepstow, in 1975, Kipper Lynch won a race on *Cantlie* with a dog never far away. Also at Chepstow, in the 1936 Welsh Grand National, a Labrador dog ran across the first open ditch and caused four fallers.

The 3.35 race at Redcar on Wednesday 16 July 1969 was the Player's Gold Leaf Filter Virginia Stakes, in the days when jokes about 'hot tips' and betting with coupons were still reasonably novel. John Player and Son put up £1,000 for the race, and four runners set off to cover 1½ miles.

Lady Anna led for a furlong, then *Javatina*, the 2–1 favourite. With 4 furlongs to go, *Lady Anna* was closely following *Javatina* and an interesting race was in prospect. About 2 furlongs out, the dogs arrived.

Dogs usually know a good horse when they can chase after it, and typically they chose to hamper the favourite more than *Lady Anna* (starting price 5–2). There were two dogs, and one crossed in front of *Lady Anna* so that it was in front of *Javatina*. The other dog turned back for the safety of the rails.

For a moment it looked as though there was danger of the dog getting among the legs of the favourite and bringing him down, but Willie Carson, on *Javatina*, helped his horse to a bit of bobbing and weaving, not to mention swerving and swearing. The race was lost – *Javatina* finished third to *Lady Anna* and *Brython* – but Carson and his mount avoided serious trouble. Indeed, there have been cases of jockeys and horses being seriously injured in such circumstances. One was Charlie Manser, at Derby in the late 19th century. A dog brought down his horse, and several other horses galloped over him.

AN ATTACK
ON THE TIERCÉ
AUTEUIL, FRANCE, DECEMBER 1973

The Prix Bride Abattue had 24 runners, and, more importantly, it qualified for the national Tiercé. This state-run betting scheme allowed punters to select the first three home.

At around 11 o'clock on the morning of the big steeplechase, it became clear to the authorities that something untoward was being organised. A lot of money was suddenly being placed on nine unfavoured horses. By 4p.m., the time of the race, the organisers were ready to observe the actual race very closely, just in case anything was amiss.

Within 300 yards (274m) of the start of the race it was apparent that it was a strange one. Two groups of horses were forming. In the leading group were the nine unfavoured horses subjected to late betting. The more laggardly group included the favourites, and it was quickly noted that the jockeys in this group tended to be linked to the same jump-training centre.

The first three horses past the post had starting prices of 31–1, 31–4 and 24–1, and anyone selecting the correct three on the Tiercé would win 13,468 francs for a three-franc bet. The alert organisers, however, immediately laid an embargo on the payment of winnings. Detectives became embroiled in the web of alleged deceit. Almost five years later, 13 jockeys, one former jockey and 40 punters were put on trial for conspiracy to defraud the public. But people were still asking who was the brains behind the scheme.

AN OUTSIDE CHANCE

LONGCHAMP, FRANCE, OCTOBER 1975

Twenty-four horses had their energy unwound at exactly 4.36p.m. The Prix de l'Arc de Triomphe was 1½ miles, two and a half minutes of intensity, and this year there were no truly outstanding horses, no *Mill Reef*, *Rheingold* or *Allez France* at their peak.

Allez France was there again, but now five years old. *Comtesse de Loir* and *Kamaraan* had been in the first four the previous year, so had to be considered, *Bruni*, winner of the St Leger by 10 lengths, was in the field, as was *Ivanjica*, another fancied horse.

Yet, despite this range of talent, some wise men of racing were debating whether this could be the year for an upset, something to rival *Topyo* in 1967 or *Levmoss* in 1969. It seemed very unlikely, but some buffeting early in the race helped cause confusion. *Dahlia* lost 10 lengths when colliding with another horse, while *Allez France* and *Ivanjica* were also badly knocked about.

Lying an unhandy 22nd out of 24, halfway through the race, was an unfancied outsider, the 119–1 *Star Appeal*. Owned by Waldemar Zeitelhack from Nuremberg, trained near Cologne by Theo Grieper, *Star Appeal* was ridden by Greville Starkey, who received his orders from the Germans via an interpreter.

Many jockeys, in Starkey's hopeless back position on an outsider, would have settled for a comfortable ride, especially in their first Arc, but Starkey felt the horse wanting to run. Starting at a 45-degree angle to the rails, he chose a wavering course through the field. Three furlongs from home, *Nobiliary* took the lead from *Citoyen*, but Starkey somehow found a way through between *Comtesse de Loir* and *Nobiliary* and came with amazing acceleration. *Star Appeal*'s appearance at the front was greeted with a roar from the crowd rather like the sound of one-hand clapping. What the hell was a 119–1 outsider doing at the front of the field and pulling away?

Amid deafening silence, the blinkered *Star Appeal* pulled away to win by three lengths from *On My Way*, *Comtesse de Loir* and *Un Kopeck*, with the unfortunately baulked *Allez France* fifth. Not surprisingly, *Star Appeal* was the longest-priced winner in the race's history.

With hindsight there were perhaps a few pointers, like the average-class field, and *Star Appeal*'s 20–1 success in the Eclipse Stakes at Sandown in July (although the horse was unplaced in the King George VI and Queen Elizabeth Diamond Stakes). But none of the tipsters had foreseen the remotest possibility of the horse being placed in, let alone winning, the Prix de l'Arc de Triomphe, and Greville Starkey was able to live out many people's dream.

MY KENTUCKY DERBY

LOUISVILLE, KENTUCKY, MAY 1976

Television companies, with their fear of static news, have upgraded what is considered strange. As individuals, however, our first experience of anything may be strange, whether it be our first race meeting, our first winner, our first visit to Hexham or whatever. Here I include a new experience of mine, to serve as a gentle reminder that *you* will have *your* own strange races, personal and precious to *you*, but I don't know about them, just as you didn't know about mine.

I arrived in Louisville late in the afternoon and walked to Churchill Downs. Had to walk. Everyone connected with transport was already at the racetrack, waiting for the 5.38 race – the Kentucky Derby. The shops had shut at 4p.m., the whole of Louisville had closed down, so I walked 4 miles (6.4km) through a modern industrial ghost city. The impact of the race was becoming clear.

At Churchill Downs, only the non-racing people were left outside, except for those standing on house roofs for a view of the track. The souvenir-vendor was packing away his toy horses. 'My next stop is the Indianapolis 500,' he told me. The woman on the next stall had sold out of lucky flowers.

On that quiet traders' corner, outside a packed stadium, I met a girl with black hair and wide-awake Panamanian eyes. In a soothing Mid-West drawl, she told me about her automobile accident and how she was too late to meet her friends. We stood in peace outside Churchill Downs minutes before the start of the big race. Inside was a seething mass of 115,000 people. The cost to join them was $10 and the loss of our privacy.

We walked around Churchill Downs, to the gate offering a view of the distant racecourse. A small crowd gathered with us, local people and shopkeepers, and someone read the odds with binoculars. A 30-year regular remarked that they opened the gates just before the big race, which they did, shortly after the singing of 'My Old Kentucky Home'. We ran across the open space to watch the Kentucky Derby for free, and for about two minutes, my friend and I took our eyes off each other to shriek with the rest as splashes of colour zipped past our noses. *Bold Forbes* held off the favourite *Honest Pleasure* for virtually all the 1¼ miles – half a length at first, a length at the most, half a length at the last.

We also saw the smoke bomb. A Kentucky National Guardsman called Barry Wall ran on to the track and rescued it like a tennis ballboy. He was later commended by many, including the Police Chief, for 'possibly saving the lives of the jockeys and horses in the race'.

The race over, peak excitement subsiding, we stumbled through the crowded infield, wading through discarded leaflets, empty cans, used newspapers and Kentucky Fried Chicken cardboard. The party-goers carried coolers and ice buckets, sleeping bags and tents. Hunter Thompson once called the infield a 'boiling sea of people'. 'It's a fantastic scene,' Thompson wrote, 'thousands of people fainting, crying, copulating, trampling each other and fighting with broken whisky bottles.'

I had underestimated the event, and I was overwhelmed by the Kentuckiana accent. 'You all come back,' the locals said, but some visitors didn't even leave, some stayed the rest of their lives. It's a strange race that affects a life. I left Louisville in August of that year.

THE GREAT AMERICAN HORSE RACE

NEW YORK STATE TO CALIFORNIA, MAY TO SEPTEMBER 1976

When Americans celebrate they do it with scale. Among the Bicentennial celebration events was the Great American Horse Race, an attempt to recapture the spirit of the great American trek from east coast to west. It was a race of 3,200 miles (5,150km), from Frankfort (New York) to Sacramento (California), through the hills of New York State, the farmlands of the Mid-West, across the Donner and Oregon trails and along the route taken by the Pony Express. As one competitor reviewed the race at the end, it was 'the damnedest test of horseflesh and people's dedication to challenge'. The most remarkable thing was that the 3,200-mile horse race was won by a 60-year-old man who had no horse.

The 91 riders represented eight different countries, and each competitor was allowed to ride only two animals. On each of 98 days they would ride approximately 35 miles, and the riders' time from start to finish of each leg was noted. An entourage of wives, husbands, lovers, relatives, supporters and veterinarians came with them, and each day the convoy moved west with the riders' tents and possessions, evoking memories of mobile villages on the great American treks of the past, albeit with cars, buses and recreation vehicles this time rather than wagons.

The first prize was worth $25,000 (£15,000), with a further $25,000 to be divided between the next nine finishers.

Towards halfway in the race, somewhere around Hannibal (Missouri), the sponsors withdrew, but the riders were so committed to the adventure – and the relationships they were forming at night – that they organised their own co-operative to see through the event. One competitor helped his expenses by selling belt buckles, buttons, shirts and other souvenirs of the race – a reminder why the Bicentennial was known by some as the 'buy-centennial'.

The big family trekked on through 13 states, although they were not welcome everywhere they went. Of the 91 riders setting out from Frankfort, 54 finished the course in Sacramento. Five out of the first ten finishers were women, but the winner was Virl Norton, a 60-year-old steeplejack from San Jose (California).

Norton had covered the 3,200 miles in the lowest aggregate time (315.47 hours) and he had achieved it without a horse. The San Jose steeplejack came home riding *Leroy* – a mule. His other mule, *Lady Eloise*, had been scratched in Nevada.

The race achieved its object of reliving the experience of American ancestors and suffering some of the same horseback hardships. The riders learned a lot in terms of coping with different weather conditions and intense personal relationships. Given the sexual freedom of the 1970s, however, one suspects that some experiences along the journey were somewhat different from those of the Californian gold rushers or the characters in Steinbeck's *Grapes of Wrath*. It sounds as though the participants had enough material for a novel or three.

BATTLING JOCKEYS
WARSAW, POLAND, OCTOBER 1978

Jockeys have used every possible weapon in order to win races. They have grabbed a rival's bridle, lifted another jockey's whip when they have lost their own and used all sorts of other means, as illustrated here.

Tommy Weston, in his autobiography *My Racing Life*, tells a tale of a jockey who was replaced on a hot favourite by the trainer. Incensed by this change, robbed of an easy winner, the jockey took another ride in the race and then spent much of the course holding the favourite's tail. Most of the other jockeys couldn't ride for laughing and certainly couldn't concentrate enough to go on ahead, so the favourite was able to win after having his tail freed in the final furlong (where there were too many onlookers). The favourite's jockey still had to explain to the trainer why his mount had only got going in the last furlong.

Another tale of comical interference concerns a jockey who spotted a horse being given a doped drink before a race. 'If it's good enough for the horse, it's good enough for me,' the jockey said, taking a swig himself, but when racing neck-and-neck for the finishing-post he felt so high that he leaned sideways and threw his arms round the neck of the nearest jockey.

One of the most heated examples of rivalry, however, was that in Poland towards the end of the 1978 season. Mieczyslaw Melnicki and Andrzej Tylicki had each ridden

98 winners that season, and both had hopes of winning the championship, ideally with 100 winners. In a race for two-year-olds, they were neck and neck down the home stretch.

They were working their horses as hard as they could. The jockeys had their whips out, and were using them, first on their horses ... and then on each other. They finished first and second but were disqualified by the stewards for hitting each other with their whips. Later they were fined and suspended for the rest of the season.

ANOTHER HOAX
NEWTON ABBOT, DECEMBER 1978

At 8.15a.m. on the morning of Tuesday 5 December, someone telephoned the BBC to pass on a message about the racing at Newton Abbot that day. The caller gave the name of a course steward and explained that the Newton Abbot meeting was abandoned through freezing fog.

Coming shortly before the 8.25 radio racing bulletin, the message was very quickly passed over the air waves. Terry Wogan made three announcements to the effect of racing being cancelled at Newton Abbot.

The drivers for two trainers, Martin Tate and Derek Haydn Jones, heard the announcement, turned round their lorries and took the horses home. Having learned the 'verdict' on Newton Abbot, they switched off their radios.

Carl Nekola was amazed when he heard the announcement. As an official at Newton Abbot, he knew it wasn't true. The meeting was still on. He telephoned the BBC, and at 8.45 Terry Wogan gave out the correct information with an apology.

This was the latest in a series of hoaxes. At 8a.m. on Thursday 30 November, the meeting at Haydock Park had been wrongly announced as abandoned. At 11a.m. on Monday 4 December, Radio Nottingham incorrectly announced no racing at Southwell. Attendances suffered at both these meetings.

The message that the Newton Abbot programme was

abandoned was eminently believable. With Wetherby abandoned through fog, Newton Abbot proved to be the only meeting taking place that day. In fact, racing started at 12.45 and the going was good.

The hoaxer left an impact. Course officials estimated that attendance was about 20 per cent below expected, eight runners were missing from the card and several of the gate staff and catering staff failed to turn up. In addition, the Racing Information Bureau and the BBC sat down to arrange a more foolproof system for conveying information on the day's race meetings.

The nature of horse racing has always left it subject to bogus information, particularly about the form of horses. Only occasionally does the hoaxer aim at institutions such as the BBC or, as we saw from the elaborate Trodmore Races hoax, the press. In 1981, for instance, a woman telephoned Weatherbys to withdraw a horse from a race at Perth. She claimed to be the wife of the horse's owner, but a tape of the conversation later showed that she wasn't, the real owner having fortunately spotted that his horse wasn't listed in the morning newspaper. He was allowed to reinstate it.

NOT BEFORE TIME
WORCESTER, OCTOBER 1979

The problems of Worcester's first race on Tuesday 9 October demonstrate the complex organisation of race meetings. A very slight error in timing and the whole system is threatened. In this instance a void race was the outcome at Worcester.

The runners for the Severn Bridge Novices' Hurdle went to the post for a 2p.m. start. At 30 seconds after 2p.m., according to the starter's watch, set by the weighing-room clock, the horses were sent on their journey.

The race had a surprise outcome. *Quantock Mauger*, trained and ridden by Brian Forsey, came home at 33–1, a head in front of *Pure Auburn* (10–1). *Carnlea House* (11–1) was third and the favourite, *Prince Fury* (9–4), no better than fourth.

The result delighted the owner of *Quantock Mauger*, Jacqueline Langley, who would qualify for first prize of £563.40. Her husband, Bryan, had even more to gain financially. He stood to win £3,376 in bets on the horse.

Then came the bombshell.

Extel and PA Joint Service pointed out that they had timed the start of the race at 1.59 and 17 seconds by their quartz crystal clock, which was checked every day and was accurate to the second. Under racing rules 28(13) and 154(1), they were the arbiters in case of a dispute over timing and an early start meant a void race. This was the first time the

Service had arbitrated since the rule had been changed in 1977.

At 2.09 (or approximately), the course stewards announced an inquiry. At 2.33, when the runners for the second race were at the post, came the next announcement: 'After holding an inquiry the stewards were satisfied that the race was started 43 seconds before its advertised time and had no alternative but to declare it void.' In Scotland, where there were more strict 'first past the post' rules, bets were likely to hold.

The Langleys were understandably frustrated and angry at the loss of their winnings, while jockey-trainer Brian Forsey was philosophical, indicating that there was nothing anyone could do about it.

The cause of the bad timing was the weighing-room clock. It was set by telephoning the speaking-clock between 8.30 and 9a.m. and checked twice before racing began. After the inquiry, the clock was shown to be 90 seconds fast, presumably because the hand had jumped. The starter had set his watch by the weighing-room clock, as he was instructed to do.

The matter did not end there. A few days later, the Worcester Racing Committee, without admitting liability, agreed to make an *ex-gratia* payment of £616 in lieu of winnings – £419 to the first placed, £133 to the second and £64 to the third. The precedent for this was probably the Valley Gardens Handicap Hurdle at Ascot in November 1969 when the owners with the winning horses threatened legal action until they were given the prize money. A start three minutes before time had caused a void race.

There are other instances. A 1962 race at Plumpton was declared void, and the following year, in June 1962, the Usk Plate at Chepstow was started four minutes early. It was rerun after the last race of the day but three runners withdrew, resulting in a walk-over. At Thirsk, in July 1988, the result of the Yorkshire Handicap looked under threat after a start nine seconds before time, but there was a sensible 15-second leeway allowed in the rules, so the result held good.

In racing's earlier days, the timing of races was not so refined, but there are countless examples of starters allowing horses to 'jump the flag'. At Newmarket in 1864, for example, a three-horse race started with only one horse at the post. Two jockeys, Wells on *Argonaut* and Adams on *Exchequer*, complained that they were a long way behind the starting-post when Mr McGeorge gave the signal for the race to begin. *Lord Burleigh*, ridden by Fordham, cantered home by 10 lengths, but the race was rerun. Such flying starts received more indignant responses on those rare occasions, those very rare occasions, when the starter seemed to have a slight connection, some remote familiarity, with the owner of the horse who was given the good start. Slowly, there evolved a complex set of rulings to ensure the neutrality and fairness of starting races and betting before them rather than during them. Not before time, people said.

THREE RACES IN ONE
CHELTENHAM, OCTOBER 1979

The Nicholson Opportunity Handicap Hurdle had nine runners, and none of the jockeys walked the course in advance of the race. The jockeys were so confused during the race that they split into three groups and set off in different directions in search of the correct course.

They were all together in a bunch at the top of Prestbury Park Hill. There, they had the choice of sticking left-handed to the inner hurdle course or going straight on to the outer course. They continued straight, and a few jockeys were surprised when they travelled some distance without a hurdle. Four took their mounts on to the end of that course, two went back to the junction, two went partway back and cut through to the old course, and one pulled out of the race altogether. I'll deal with them one race at a time.

The four who stuck to the new, outer course reached the finishing-post first but found only one hurdle on the rest of their journey. *Tyrullah* led the group but made a mistake at the hurdle and slipped back. *Gin 'n Lime* passed the post first, in front of *Tempest Girl*. The two 9–4 co-favourites, *Tyrullah* and *Wheel-em-Boy*, finished third and fourth in that race.

Historic Myth and *Hardivim* retraced their tracks, turned left by the farm and reappeared at the 2-mile start, back on the correct course. They raced each other, and *Historic Myth* won that one. That left the third race, between *Hanley Swan* and *Dante's Rogue*, these two horses retracing their steps further back than the others. Paul Carvill, on *Dante's Rogue*, was still not sure of the course, so he waited for James Darlington on *Hanley Swan* and then the two set off on their race. *Hanley Swan* led down the hill, over the three hurdles they found on their course and past the finishing-post. Meanwhile, the ninth horse in the race, *Tim Ding*, had been pulled up, but even his associates had hope of a favourable result, perhaps a void race.

The winners of the three heats passed the finishing-post in the order of *Gin 'n Lime*, *Historic Myth* and *Hanley Swan*. Seven horses made their way to the winner's enclosure, just in case, and the bookies accepted 1–4 on *Historic Myth* and 2–1 on *Hanley Swan* for the Nicholson Opportunity Handicap Hurdle. The odds on *Hanley Swan* quickly shortened to 1–5 as word went round, and, sure enough, James Darlington's mount was given the race. The jockey recognised that it was his lucky day; eight horses to beat, and four went the wrong way, one pulled up, two went wrong again and the other waited for him to catch up.

Six horses were disqualified – the four who continued on the new course and jumped only one more hurdle, and the two who cut through to the correct course without retracing their steps far enough. *Hanley Swan* (16–1) and *Dante's Rogue* (33–1) were adjudged the only two finishers.

A similar mistake at Wincanton five days previously (5 October) saw the first four disqualified for taking the wrong course, so stern warnings were issued to ensure that jockeys familiarised themselves with the course before a race. At Cheltenham, the jockeys were shown the course on a map in the weighing-room, but that was no substitute for walking the course, even though it was no different to that of previous years. No disciplinary action was taken over the incident, because the horses were so bunched when they went wrong, but dolls were put out to exaggerate the course markings, just to make sure there was no repetition of the confusion among jockeys that afternoon.

RERUN RACE AT RIPON

RIPON, AUGUST 1980

There were 14 runners for the Yorkshire Handicap, the 4.30 flat race at Ripon on 4 August, and only eight finished. Bookmakers were thrown into confusion by the events, and controversy continued for days, so much so that some punters referred to it as the 'Ripon rip-off'.

The start was fair, but, 1 furlong down the 6-furlong course, Ernie Green waved his red flag as if to indicate a false start. A human error. Six jockeys brought their mounts to a halt. They included Eddie Hide on the 4–1 favourite *Swaying Tree* and Paul Cook on *Lost for Words*, a horse appropriately named for the occasion. Further down the course, C. Storey took *Wynburry* on to beat *Another Venture* by three-quarters of a length.

At 4.35 came the first announcement – that the race was void. At 4.48 came a contradictory announcement – that the race had a false start. At 5.04 came another announcement that the race would be rerun at 5.30.

But what were the bookmakers to do? If it were a void race then money should be returned to the betters, and some had started to do this. If the race was rerun, then original starting prices would hold. Or should they open up a new book?

The debate, like the race, would run and run.

Nine owners were given permission to withdraw their horses from the field for the 5.30 rerun, and that left only five runners. Then came two other unusual events. Eddie

Hide, who had weighed out on *Swaying Tree*, had gone to hospital as a precaution after being kicked by a horse while waiting for the stewards' decision, so Jimmy Bleasdale replaced him as *Swaying Tree*'s jockey. And then the horses were put into adjacent starting-stalls rather than the ones they had used at 4.30.

The rerun race created further problems with its outcome. *Lost for Words* led until headed by *Wynburry*, who, in turn, was replaced by *Gin Game*. Then *Swaying Tree* came with a late run to win by one and a half lengths. This perhaps wasn't surprising. Eddie Hide had pulled up *Swaying Tree* an hour before, whereas *Wynburry* and *Gin Game* had been forced to go the 6-furlong distance at full speed.

The series of events were subjected to various bookmakers' interpretations. Some bookmakers accepted the *Sporting Life* judgment that money should be paid at the original starting prices and betters whose horses were absent from the second race could not claim refunds. Other bookmakers stuck to the original 'void race' announcement and claimed that the rerun race was in fact a new race with a new book suiting the field of five.

All this tested the tempers of some punters. There were those who had reclaimed their money on *Swaying Tree* after the race had been declared void and now, when the horse had come up, they had no ticket. There were those who had bet on *Wynburry* at 14–1 and reckoned they deserved something for winning the first race at 4.30. There were those who had bet before 4.30 but were given a later starting price on *Swaying Tree* (6–5) rather than the original 4–1 starting price. And there were those whose horses had been absent from the rerun race and who couldn't claim back their stake (although in fact many bookmakers refunded this money).

Edith Kettlewell, the owner of *Wynburry*, planned to appeal to the Jockey Club, but withdrew when she learned that the Jockey Club were launching an inquiry anyway.

It took place on 12 August, eight days after the race. The Jockey Club stewards ruled that, given the 'exceptional circumstances', the course stewards were entitled to conclude a false start and order a rerun of the race, and neither the replacement of a jockey nor the mix-up over starting-stalls invalidated the result. Surprising to some, no action was taken against the course stewards, although it was recognised that communication had been poor, and it was pointed out that the rerun should have taken place immediately.

So the racing outcome was a victory for *Swaying Tree*, which enabled an interesting piece of history to be created. How many other horses have won a race with one jockey aboard at the off and another at the finish?

ALDANITI AT AINTREE
AINTREE, LIVERPOOL, APRIL 1981

It was more than enough to move a nation. The story of the run-in for the 1981 Grand National involved a jockey who had recovered from cancer, a lightly raced horse who had missed the best part of three years with crippling injuries and a 54-year-old who had bred, owned, trained and ridden the favourite. In the background were a wealth of caring people who made it all possible. No wonder the film *Champions* was made.

At the start of 1979 Bob Champion was a fit and healthy 30-year-old jockey with almost 350 winners. He had no need to look further than the next ride ... until he was told that he had cancer and no longer than eight months to live without intensive, radical treatment.

He underwent an operation to remove part of a rib and a testicle (where the trouble had started after he had received a ferocious kick while remounting a horse in a race). The operation was followed by six 21-day cycles of chemotherapy treatment with its associated side-effects, such as loss of hair.

Champion left the Royal Marsden Hospital in Surrey on New Year's Day 1980. He was thin, wasted and light on muscles. Slowly, stubbornly, he worked himself back to health. One thing that helped him was the prospect of riding *Aldaniti* in the 1980 Grand National, an ambition considered wildly optimistic, all the more since the horse trained by Josh Gifford and owned by Nick Embiricos was suffering too.

Aldaniti, named after breeder Tommy Barron's four grandchildren (Alistair, David, Nicola and Timothy), had a history of leg injuries. Foaled in 1970, he missed virtually all of two separate years (1976 and 1978) before breaking down for the third time on the off fore leg during a race at Sandown in November 1979.

The horse's recovery time was as long as Bob Champion's, but horse and jockey were together again to win the Whitbread Trial Handicap Chase in February 1981. This was *Aldaniti*'s only race in the 16 months before the 1981 *Sun* Grand National.

The favourite for the race was John Thorne's *Spartan Missile*. The breeder-owner-trainer-rider had wasted hard to make a reasonable weight, conceding 6lb (2.7kg) to the favourably handicapped *Aldaniti*. At the age of 54, in his 32nd riding season, Thorne had his best chance of winning the Grand National. *Spartan Missile* had already finished fourth in the Cheltenham Gold Cup that year.

Bob Champion had a poor record in the Grand National in the 1970s. Although he had twice finished sixth, he had also twice fallen at the first fence. Gifford and Champion agreed that *Aldaniti* should run a waiting race on the safe ground on the outside, but the start was auspicious. *Aldaniti* did well to regain his balance after almost falling at the first and he scraped his belly on the second. By the fifth he was jumping beautifully and, after Canal Turn, Champion let the horse take him to the front, despite the agreement to hang back.

At the last fence, *Aldaniti* led from *Royal Mail* and *Spartan Missile*. John Thorne's horse, 10 lengths behind the leader on landing, made a valiant effort in the long run-in, overhauling *Royal Mail* and, 100 yards (91.4m) out, closing to within three lengths of a very tired *Aldaniti*. But Champion cracked the whip, *Aldaniti* responded, and the horse and jockey came home to complete a fairy tale. Second-placed Thorne was the first to pat Champion on the back.

Tragically, John Thorne was killed in a racing fall in March 1982. And there was to be no Grand National repeat for *Aldaniti* and Bob Champion in 1982, when the horse fell at the first fence. It was the horse's first fall in 28 races in what proved to be his last race. But *Aldaniti* didn't retire easily. He returned to play himself (with the help of six doubles) in the film *Champions*, while John Hurt played Bob Champion.

A HELICOPTER TREBLE

SANDOWN, BATH AND NOTTINGHAM, JULY 1981

As an example of the strange, busy life led by jockeys, we can take a look at a day in the career of Paul Cook. At the time he was 35 years old, experienced and professional enough to be in demand. He needed to be in two or three places at once, and, on Saturday 4 July, he came very close.

On the day before, Paul Cook had ridden a treble – *Norwick* in the 3.15 at Haydock Park, *Goldliner Abbey* in the 6.45 at Beverley, and *Chester County* in the 7.10 at Beverley. Also that Friday, Cook had ridden a third in the 8.35 at Beverley and had been unplaced in a race at each of his venues.

The Saturday, though, was busier still. He started at Sandown Park (Surrey), where he was unplaced in the first race at 1.45. In the second race, the 2.15, he led on *Princes Gate* from a furlong out and won by three-quarters of a length at 6–1. From Sandown he set off for Bath by helicopter – a distance of about 90 miles (145km).

Cook arrived at Bath in good time for the 4.30 race, in which he was unplaced on *Another Way*, and then won the last race on the card, the 5p.m. race, on *Ramannolie* at 11–4. He hadn't gone all that way for nothing, as astute punters often notice. And next he was off to Nottingham – this time a helicopter ride of about 120 miles (193km).

Paul Cook arrived at Nottingham racecourse in time to ride in four races. He was unplaced on *Orley's Farm* in the 7.25, but won on 5–2 favourite *Pavilion* in the 7.50.

Like his other two winners that day, *Pavilion* was trained by Tom Jones. Unlike the other two winners, this one was watched by Jones, whose assistant had accompanied the horses to Sandown and Bath. Paul Cook's rides in the 8.40 and the 9.05 at Nottingham failed to gain a place, but his day had brought him eight rides, three winners and a lot of travelling.

Cook's experience that day somehow symbolises the mobility of the modern-day professional jockey. In the past, jockeys were accustomed to racing around between races but not to such a dramatic extent. In October 1952, for instance, T. Shone, a National Hunt jockey, received some incredulous reactions after a car dash across the Midlands. He weighed in after winning the 2.30 race at Southwell, threw a coat over his jockey's clothes, collected his bag, ran to his car and drove 42 miles (67.6km) to Uttoxeter to ride in the 4.30 Ashbourne Steeplechase.

Some things, however, don't change. In the unlikely event of anyone advertising for jockeys, the qualities and skills would not have varied much in post-war years. Lightly built person required for hard, physical, dangerous work with long hours. Must have an affinity with animals, a passion for open-air work ... and a desire to travel. High rewards for a high achiever.

A BALLOT FOR WHO RACES
BRIGHTON, AUGUST 1981

Sadly, the death of a jockey after a fall in a race is too common an occurrence to warrant the category of 'strange race' – deaths have averaged almost one a year in the post-war period – but the reaction to the death of a flat-race jockey can create a peculiar event, as happened in August 1981.

A reminder that horse-riding can be a lethal form of transport came on 8 July 1981, when *Sleigh Queen*, ridden by Joe Blanks from Ryan Price's Findon stable, clipped the heels of another horse just before the 3-furlong pole in the Rock Garden Maiden Stakes at Brighton. The horse fell, and several horses appeared to gallop over Blanks, who required artificial respiration before being taken to Royal Sussex Hospital with head and chest injuries. Sadly, the 24-year-old jockey died eight days later without regaining consciousness.

Blanks's death led to an outcry over safety at a time when jockeys' injuries seemed more numerous than usual. The courses were running fast, but that was no explanation for the bizarre starting-stall accident to Lester Piggott. And there were some who fervently believed that the flat race in which Joe Blanks was fatally injured was too densely populated with 20 horses. When the jockeys returned to Brighton, they threatened action unless the numbers in a race were reduced.

Brighton had had a 24-horse limit in operation for 29 years. At the time of the Blanks tragedy the limit was reduced to 22 because of a temporary running-rail that was in place on the course. When this rail was removed, in time for the August meeting, the limit was back at 24.

The Hassocks Maiden Stakes on 5 August was run over the same 6-furlong course as that of the Rock Garden Maiden Stakes, the race in which Joe Blanks had received his fatal injuries. The jockeys made it clear that they would not ride unless a lower limit was imposed. Rather than split the race, the authorities decided to hold a ballot at Brighton on the day of the race, 45 minutes before the race was due to start. They would reduce the 22 entries to 16. As there was one non-runner, *Eagle Quest*, five horses were actually drawn from the ballot-box, or, rather, withdrawn from the ballot-box.

Although most of the jockeys were pleased at the reduction, the method raised a few eyebrows. What about the expenses of bringing horses from places like Newmarket and then having the course stewards declare them non-runners, as happened in two cases? One owner had taken a day off from his business and travelled for two and a half hours to see his horse. Fortunately, that one made the cut.

The Hassocks Maiden Stakes was won by Graham Sexton on *Opal Lady*.

A TALE OF TWO GREYS
LEICESTER, MARCH 1982

The first race on the card at Leicester on 29 March, the Knighton Auction Stakes, was won by a grey horse. That much is known. But the identity of the horse is another matter.

Among the ten runners listed for the Knighton Auction Stakes, a race for two-year-olds, was *Flockton Grey*, a grey gelding by *Dragonara Palace* and *Misippus*, a horse supposedly in the charge of trainer Stephen Wiles. The horse, or what people presumed to be the horse, romped home to win by 20 lengths at 10–1, a victory so easy that both jockey Kevin Darley and trainer Wiles were taken by surprise.

Bookmakers were also surprised, so much so that a few suspected a ruse. The eventual investigations, taking nearly five years, concluded that the winner of the 1982 Knighton Auction Stakes was in fact *Good Hand*, a three-year-old grey, a better and more experienced runner than *Flockton Grey*.

In May and June 1984 three men were subjected to a five-week trial in York, charged with conspiracy to defraud bookmakers by switching horses. The men in the dock were Kenneth Richardson, 47, chairman of East Riding Paper Sack Company, a wealthy self-made businessman and racehorse owner who was alleged to have 'masterminded' the fraud, Richardson's racing manager Colin Mathison and his horsebox driver Peter Boddy. In police custody were two horses. *Good Hand* had been found in a field at Glaisdale in North Yorkshire, and *Flockton Grey* in a stable near Wakefield.

The prosecution showed that *Flockton Grey* had been previously taken away from the horse's trainer, contrary to rule 184(a) which stipulated that a horse should be in the care of a licensed trainer for the 14 days before a race. The trainer, Stephen Wiles, admitted that he had seen the horse only briefly before it left his charge and appeared (supposedly) at Leicester with identification papers for an unnamed two-year-old. However, photographs of the winning Leicester horse suggested the teeth of a *three-*year-old, while Colin Tinkler recognised the pictures as those of *Good Hand*, a horse he had trained at Malton before selling to Colin Mathison, one of the defendants. On the other hand, the defence produced witnesses to suggest that the photographs weren't conclusive and a veterinary surgeon had failed to identify the Leicester entry as a three-year-old.

The prosecution claimed that the three men had made £36,000 from a betting coup before the race, but Richardson argued in his defence that this was a small amount compared with his normal betting winnings and his business dealings. After the jury had been out for eight hours, they reached a majority verdict in the prosecution's favour. Kenneth Richardson received a nine-month sentence, suspended for a year, and was fined £20,000, plus £100,000 costs and, two years later, when the appeal failed, further costs of not more than £25,000. Mathison was fined £3,000 and Boddy received a 12-month conditional discharge.

The trainer of the 'ringer' horse, *Good Hand*, was not identified at the trial. The two horses, the chief exhibits, were kept in police custody for almost five years at a cost to the taxpayer of about £10,000. Eventually, *Flockton Grey* was sold for 680 guineas to a trainer, Robin Bastiman, who bought him for a client. That was in December 1986, when the horse was a seven-year-old and still to run a race.

All that remained was for the Jockey Club to bestow its own sentences – a five-year disqualification and the loss of his trainer's licence for Stephen Wiles, a 25-year ban for Kenneth Richardson, 15 years for Colin Mathison and three years for Peter Boddy.

The *Flockton Grey* case is far from the only example of horse-switching in racing history. The winner of a race at Stockton in 1919 was actually *Jaz* rather than *Coat of Bail*, so one man went to gaol. *Stellar City* was substituted for *Peaceful William* in 1949 and two men received 18-month gaol sentences. *Francasal* was replaced by *Santa Amaro* in 1953 (see page 127) and four men received sentence terms of between nine months and three years. In 1974 there was horse-play involving *Gay Future* and a bogus *Gay Future* at Cartmel, so two men found guilty were fined £1,000 (plus costs) and one of them, a Scottish trainer, received a ten-year disqualification. *In the Money* was replaced by *Cobblers March* at Newton Abbot in 1978, leading to an 18-month suspended sentence for one man and a £1,500 fine (plus costs) plus 20-year disqualification for a trainer. And these are only some of the incidents that have gone to court.

More recently, there was an Australian outcry in December 1984, when four bookmakers and a Roman Catholic priest were among eight people banned from racecourses for life after a multi-million dollar betting fraud involving the switching of *Bold Personality* for *Fine Cotton* in a race the previous August. One recalls the words of John Fairfax-Blakeborough's *Memoirs*: 'It has been proved beyond all doubt that to be successful as a scoundrel on the turf a man must either work single-handed or must have accomplices who are deaf, dumb, unable to write and without any memory.'

A WIN FOR A RIDERLESS HORSE

SIENA, ITALY, JULY 1983

I once asked a friend what he thought would be first past the post in the forthcoming Grand National.

'Riderless horse,' he answered.

Flippant he may have been, but, nevertheless, a riderless horse has in recent years won one of Europe's most famous horse races, and the result stood.

The *Corsa del Palio*, raced in Siena since 1659, is a central feature of one of Northern Italy's most famous festivals. The structure of the race originated in the ancient administrative divisions of Siena. The three main regions, the *Terzi*, are subdivided into *Contrade*, which are like wards or parishes. There is intense rivalry between the *Contrade* and, twice a year, on 2 July and 16 August, representatives of 10 *Contrade* are chosen to race bareback on horses around the main square of Siena. The ten will include the seven not represented in the last *Palio*, plus three other *Contrade* drawn by lots.

The main square, the *piazza del campo*, is not, strictly speaking, a square. It is shaped like a scallop, in a slight arc on one side and straight on the opposite edge. The chosen jockeys need a few rehearsals, including one on the morning of the race. The jockeys and horses are blessed, and a parade acts as the prelude to the big race. Wearing medieval costume, the jockeys race in the early evening. The prize is the *palio*, a banner bearing the effigy of the

Virgin, the protectress of Siena. The winning jockey does not win the *palio* for himself.

He wins it for his *Contrade*. The race, which lasts for only a minute, is an intense climax to the festival.

The regional rivalry manifests itself in fanatical support and extensive betting. Spectators wedged in the middle of the square, inside the historic racecourse, gladly suffer hot and crowded conditions. Privileged spectators watch from the balconies of buildings overlooking the square. As the jockeys negotiate the dangers of the course – three laps of the square with sharp turns at the corners – the crowd yell and shout. In 1983 they did more than just yell. They fought over the result.

The cause for complaint that year was the controversial finish. Veteran jockey Giuseppe Pes looked like riding the favourite to victory. It looked even more certain when Silvano Vigni was unseated from *Benito*, the horse lying second. Yet when *Benito* picked up pace, took the lead and was first past the post, the riderless horse was not disqualified but given the race. The reason was quite simple. The original rules of the race stated that a horse need not carry a rider to win.

A NATIONAL HUNT WORLD CHAMPIONSHIP
CHELTENHAM, APRIL 1984

Twelve jockeys arrived from 12 different countries, ready to ride for points to decide the first National Hunt world championship. Four races were arranged, and the idea was to have 12 runners in each, and for each trainer to draw a jockey by lottery. The scoring system was 10 points for a win, seven for second place, four for third and two for fourth. No more than the three best places could count for each jockey, a rule to compensate for some jockeys being left without a ride in the third race, which was light on entries.

The event was sponsored by Railfreight, and the four races were all given suitable Railfreight names – the Freight Train Hurdle, the Speedlink Distribution Hurdle, the Railfreight Chase and the Speedlink International Novice Hurdle.

The draw was lucky to John Francome, and the general opinion was that the British jockey would ride favourites to victory in the first two races to build up an unassailable championship lead. In the first race, Francome rode the 8–1 *Don Giovanni*, a horse he had twice ridden to victory already that season, but the xenophobes in the crowd were surprised by the riding performance of a 33-year-old Japanese jockey called Shinobu Hoshino. *Desert Hero*, the 10–1 shot from Fulke Walwyn's stable, had never jumped better than he did for Hoshino. Carrying 8st (50.8kg) of the jockey and more than 3st (19kg) of lead to make up the weight, *Desert Hero* pipped *Don Giovanni* and gave the Japanese jockey a ten-point start.

Francome won the next race on 7–4 favourite *Fitzherbert*, and Belgian jockey Phillip Caus put in a good ride on *Greenwood Lad* to take the third race. Three jockeys fell in that race, which led to Peter Scudamore winning the final race of the championship as a substitute.

John Francome collected 17 points, which was enough to take the championship from Phillip Caus (14), Gianantonio Colleo of Italy (13) and Shinobu Hoshino (10). The first prize was £2,500 and a Philip Blacker bronze.

A PHOTO-FINISH ...
BETWEEN FOOT AND
GROUND

NEWTON ABBOT, AUGUST 1984

It was a novice chase with all the associated unpredictable behaviour. Of the seven runners, *First Award* fell at the seventh, bringing down *Brianka*, *Gamel's Path* went at the 13th, and *Free Drop* was pulled up lame. That left three, one of whom, *Legal Session*, fell at the second last and had to be remounted.

Tango Shandy (8–1) reached the last fence with lengths to spare over the 25–1 outsider *Cold View*. Then came trouble. *Tango Shandy* recovered well enough after making a mistake at the fence, but the horse's saddle slipped. Stuart Kittow, *Tango Shandy*'s 6ft 3in (1m 91cm) amateur jockey, lost his irons but performed incredibly well on the run-in. Kittow held on to the horse's neck as the saddle slipped off the horse's back, clinging desperately to the reins as *Tango Shandy* neared the winning-post and Kittow's feet slid towards the ground. Around the finishing-line, his feet touched the ground and he was dragged along for 20 yards (18.3m) before bringing his mount to a stop. He was fit enough to weigh in and acknowledge the applause of the spectators, who appreciated his improvised heroics.

The judge awarded the race to *Tango Shandy* and Stuart Kittow, but, 15 minutes after the finish, a stewards' inquiry was announced. The matter under scrutiny was whether Kittow's foot had touched the ground before or after the horse reached the finishing-post. The stewards studied the photo-finish photograph and decided that it was before. *Tango Shandy*'s trainer, Gerald Cottrell, studied the photograph and decided that Kittow's foot touched the ground after the line.

When the Newton Abbot stewards disqualified *Tango Shandy*, 45 minutes after the end of the race, Cottrell appealed to the Jockey Club. The stewards at Portman Square upheld the appeal and awarded the race back to *Tango Shandy*.

The race raised some interesting debate. What was this rule anyway? *Legal Session*'s jockey had touched the ground in the same race, falling and then remounting. And if Kittow was simply brushing the grass with his foot, was that acceptable?

One of Kittow's supporters pointed out that had his foot hit the ground at the angle shown in the photograph, the jockey would probably have been injured, according to expert opinion. But, to be fair to the stewards on the course, it was very difficult to tell from the evidence. As they say in America, the jury is still out.

There are other examples of saddles slipping in the home straight. Perhaps the most dramatic were a win for *Epsom Lad* in the 1901 Eclipse Stakes, jockey Gomez riding over the line while holding the saddle in place with one hand, and Willie Carson's ride into third place on *Dibidale* in the 1974 Oaks. Although Carson somehow managed to finish without the saddle hitting the floor, the weight cloth was lost and he was unable to make the weight.

GOLD SNOW

CHELTENHAM, MARCH 1987

Some race meetings in the distant past have taken place in dense fog, dangerous flooding or driving snow, as indicated in this book, whereas modern-day racecourse executives would probably abandon meetings in such conditions. Even so, today's racecourses are not short of weather, and the Cheltenham Gold Cup could act as a magnet for meteorologists. The timing of the race – close to the March equinox – guarantees a variety of weather conditions. One year they used helicopters to fan the course dry. In 1978, snow caused the big race to be delayed until the middle of April. In yet another year, the course executives were in trouble for watering the course during a drought. But the 1987 Gold Cup brought perhaps the most extreme conditions yet.

It had been promising snow all day. In fact, Cheltenham was fortunate to escape overnight snow that hit other parts of the country. When it came, though, the snow struck hard. The blizzard arrived just as the horses for the Gold Cup were parading in the ring. It was agreed to put back the race until the blizzard had cleared. The jockeys dismounted and waited.

At the first hopeful sign, the jockeys were asked to mount their horses again. They rode to the start, but the weather was no better. They returned to the parade ring and again dismounted.

It had already been an afternoon of incident – eight spectators were injured when they fell from a rooftop vantage point during the first race – and now there was more. A streaker, cold and bare, took to the course during one of the hold-ups. Not all the 48,301 spectators noticed. Some were working hard, attempting to calculate how a heavy fall of snow would affect the chances of the runners. Surely the northern horses would react better to this? Surely the temperate horses would react better to the delay, which crept up to 80 minutes?

The starting price of one northern horse, *The Thinker*, owned by three McDonagh brothers, trained by Arthur Stephenson and ridden by Ridley Lamb, came down dramatically – from 9–1 to 13–2. The trust was well-placed. Although *Cybrandian*, ridden by Chris Grant, ran well and looked like providing a surprise 25–1 winner, *The Thinker* got up to win by one and a half lengths. *Door Latch* was third at 9–1. The sun made a generous appearance, but it was still amazing that the race was run. However, if the Derby has been run in a snowstorm at least twice, in 1839 and 1898, then the Cheltenham Gold Cup is an obvious contender.

People made comparisons with St Moritz in Switzerland, where races on snowy lakes have been organised in February for much of this century, the course being reconstructed each year. St Moritz has staged an incredible variety of races, including hurdle races for amateurs, trotting horses with sleigh-bound jockeys, and galloping horses with jockeys skiing behind. Sidney Galtrey, in *Memoirs of a Racing Journalist*, offers an early description of St Moritz: 'They laid out a racecourse on the two or three feet of snow on the frozen lake, they rolled it and rolled it, put up a makeshift weighing-room of rough timber, fenced off some enclosures, and, of course, a Tote building. Horses were brought up from Zurich, some from Italy, a few from Germany.'

At St Moritz jockeys learned that being in front was useful – to save snow being thrown into your face – and trainers learned to equip their horses with studded shoes or other protective footwear. But Cheltenham in 1987 was a more surprising snowy experience.

AN ANNOUNCER'S MISTAKE

SANDOWN PARK, JUNE 1987

There is an old story of how a judge informed his assistant that number 13 had won a race, and the assistant automatically put up '14' in the frame as the winner. Not everybody's accent is easy to understand, and the human mind can drift from time to time.

Although racecourses are now extremely well organised, there is always the likelihood of someone playing the game of Chinese Whispers whereby a message starts off as one thing ('send reinforcements, we're going to advance') and ends as another ('send three and fourpence, we're going to a dance'). The 1987 Baker Lorenz Summer Handicap is a case in point.

They raced over 5 furlongs, *Duck Flight* making the early running and *Vague Lass* leading into the final furlong. The favourite *Respect* came with a strong late run to compensate for a very slow start, but no one could quite head off *Padre Pio*, a six-year-old who had only recently recovered from a broken pelvis. *Padre Pio* won by half a length at 11–4, and the judge called for a photograph to decide second place.

It took the judge only a few seconds to decide that *Respect* beat *Vague Lass* by a neck for second place, but it was more than an hour before the public knew the correct result. By then it was too late to affect the betting.

The announcer took the judge's result and got it wrong. *Vague Lass* was announced as second, *Respect* placed third.

In effect this meant *Respect* was unplaced as it was a six-horse race. It was a simple human error.

The matter was made more difficult by the location of the judge's box for the 5-furlong races at Sandown. The judge couldn't hear the announcement. He assumed it would be correct.

The mistake was not discovered until an hour later, when someone pointed out that the placings were different from those in the numbers board. As the jockeys had weighed in, it was too late to affect the betting although the prize money for second place eventually went to the owner of *Respect*.

There was almost a recurrence of the incident at Newcastle a fortnight later, when a wrong announcement for placings in the EBF Angerton Graduation Stakes was corrected in time but left punters angry at the ambiguity. And an Extel commentary announced the wrong winner for a race at Pontefract the same month, the commentator not believing that a horse could fail to win when three lengths clear nearly at the line.

On 26 June the Jockey Club acted with some more foolproof regulations. The judge would in future ask the announcer what he was going to announce, and then the judge would listen to the announcement, just to be sure.

TROUBLE AT 1 O'CLOCK
CHEPSTOW, DECEMBER 1987

It was embarrassing that the BBC cameras should capture the trouble caused by the incorrect marking of the course for the second race of the day. The jockeys did their utmost to turn the race into a viable contest but they were faced with one of the most unusual obstacles on a steeplechase course – 15 yards (13.7m) of running-rail.

The first race on the card that day – Saturday 5 December – was a flat race, and the course was correctly marked. But the dolls on the inside of the bend for the first race were left in place for the 1 o'clock race, the Prince of Wales Novices' Chase. Instead of the runners being able to take the correct course at the point where the hurdle and steeplechase courses cross, they were trapped on the hurdle course by the barriers and the running-rail. They were unable to jump the first steeplechase fence on the straight.

The favourite *Fu's Lady*, ridden by Tommy Carroll, set a brave example by attempting to jump the running-rail. He hit the 'fence', broke the rail and slipped and fell on landing. Neither horse nor jockey was injured in the incident, which was in some ways fortunate because it left a hole in the running-rail. Some of the other jockeys took their mounts through the gap, and the race – what was left of it – continued on the proper course.

Only five of the 11 starters completed the strange course. Hywel Davies came home first on *Only Trouble*, with *Top*

Gold and *Vipsania* second and third. The course steward had little option but to declare the race void and admit that the Clerk of the Course was responsible for the error. A month later the Chepstow course executive agreed to payout a share of the £230 prize money to the owners of the entered horses. The entry fees were deducted from accounts at Weatherbys.

VICTORY ... A WEEK LATER
WEXFORD, MARCH 1988

In a race where almost all the jockeys lost their way – the 3-mile Rathnure Handicap – the last horse to finish was initially given the race but the result was changed a week later.

Thirteen ran, and ten finished. On the first circuit, however, *Lady Daffydown* led the field the wrong side of a marker. Pat O'Donnell, riding *Derry Gowan*, twigged what had happened, so he took his horse back down the course and came the correct side of the marker. O'Donnell had walked the course in advance of the race. Others presumably hadn't.

Second favourite *Derry Gowan* was tenth past the winning-post, tenth out of ten finishers. A 14–1 outsider, *Sirrah Jay*, was first past the post – followed by *Let's Promise* (12–1) and *Brussels Sprouts* (6–1) – but was one of nine finishers disqualified after a very lengthy stewards' inquiry. The delay in announcing the result was partly caused by the poor view of the incident provided by the video of the race watched by the stewards. Eventually they concluded that 12 of the 13 starters – all except *Derry Gowan* – had been taken on the wrong route. *Derry Gowan* – starting price 5–1 – was declared the only finisher, which qualified the winning owner for first, second and third prizes, a total of IR£1,586.

After studying another video, which gave a better view of the marker incident, trainer Oliver Finnegan agreed with jockey Pat Malone that their horse, *Mullaghea*, had also taken the correct course. They appealed to the Irish National Hunt Committee, and the appeal was considered on 9 March, six days after the race.

The appeal was successful. *Mullaghea*, who had finished sixth, had taken the correct course, and the result was altered. *Mullaghea* was given first place, and *Derry Gowan*, who had already finished tenth and first, was now demoted to second.

This particular example of bad map-reading was one of several that winter. Besides the calamity at Chepstow in December 1987, there were errors made in the 1.45 race at Sandown Park on 14 January 1988. The wrong course was taken by six jockeys, some claiming they were blinded by the glare of the sun, and the 20 runners were whittled down by the end of the race; six were disqualified, two pulled up, two unseated their riders and one ran out.

In March 1988 Graham Bradley and Geoff Harker were both heavily fined for missing a fence and then missing a circuit of a novice steeplechase at Sedgefield. They rode a hard-fought, close finish, but with a circuit to go. And the 1988 Festival Stakes at Goodwood was another which engaged the stewards in a debate about the course actually taken.

ULTRASONIC SOUND?
ASCOT, JUNE 1988

On the Thursday of Ascot week, the racecourse was a beautiful, colourful sight. The Princess of Wales was there, wearing a grey tail coat over the top of a white blouse and white skirt. The Queen and the Duchess of York were both in deep pink. The Queen Mother wore turquoise and white, Princess Alexandra yellow and black, and the Princess Royal pink and emerald green. It was hardly a setting worthy of controversy, cocaine and conspiracy. Yet, over 16 months later, an attempt was made to link them with that Ascot day.

The race in question was the King George V Handicap, the 5.30 race that day, but it is worth mentioning in passing that the 3.45 race, the Gold Cup itself, was also a strange race. The French horse *Royal Gait* came in first by five lengths but the horse was disqualified and American jockey Cash Asmussen banned for seven days. The course stewards blamed Asmussen for a fall by Tony Clark on *El Conquistador*, an action supported later by the Jockey Club, but some thought Asmussen was harshly treated and others maintained that Greville Starkey, whose horse *Sadeem* was given the race, was as much to blame.

It was Starkey who was involved in the mysterious events of the King George V Handicap. He was riding the 4–1 favourite *Ile De Chypre*, well in the lead and entering the last furlong, when, suddenly, without warning, the horse veered sharp left and unseated Starkey. *Ile De Chypre* joined the long line of horses, including *Limerock* and *Devon Loch*, who have done something out of character when a race was well within their grasp. No one could explain the incident, but 16 months later an explanation was put forward.

On 18 October 1989, three men went on trial at Southwark Crown Court for cocaine-related offences. The prosecution spent the first few days of the case presenting the evidence against James Laming, Martin Cox and Patrick Fraser, alleging that they had been involved in a £15 million cocaine chain led by Rene Black, who had already admitted the charges. The case was of no interest to horse racing enthusiasts ... until 31 October, when Laming presented his defence.

James Laming, while admitting that he was a 'social user' of cocaine, gave evidence that his involvement with Black was not through cocaine dealing but a separate conspiracy to undermine the entire system of racecourse betting. Laming claimed he had invented a set of binoculars which transmitted 23 kilohertz noise waves – above the human hearing range of 20 kilohertz but within a horse's hearing range. The binoculars achieved this by having two high-powered ceramic transducers (loudspeakers) instead of lenses, a tiny amplifier and a cable connecting them to cadmium batteries in their case. Laming alleged that Rene Black, a wealthy Peruvian show-jumper, had staked £10,000 to develop the binoculars.

Fired at a horse from relatively short range, as it had been at Ascot by James Laming's brother Robert, the effect was literally startling. A novel sound, unheard by humans, pierced through *Ile De Chypre* and caused the horse to jink left and throw Starkey, so Laming said in evidence. The betting coup was achieved by either betting against the favourite or betting on the second favourite.

'If it worked there (Ascot) it would work anywhere,' said Cox, who organised the betting, in evidence. 'Nobody knew what happened at that race until we came into court.'

After the 'successful' trial at Ascot, the binoculars gang intended to try again at Lingfield, but Laming was arrested on 13 August 1988, before the experiment could continue.

The jury listened patiently to Laming's story, and they also listened to the prosecution's allegation that the idea was far-fetched and merely a smokescreen for the cocaine smuggling and supplying. The 12 trusted people deliberated for almost five hours. Then they announced a guilty verdict for James Laming, and not guilty for Martin Cox.

A SUDDEN FALL

DONCASTER, SEPTEMBER 1989

One of the most frightening events in horse racing is when a bunch of horses are racing on the flat at high speed, perhaps 30–35mph (48.3–56.3km/h), and something happens spontaneously – a horse is injured, two horses collide, an Emily Davison runs on the track and so on. If we consult the Highway Code's shortest stopping distances for cars at that speed – for 30mph it is 25 yards (22.9m) – we realise the sort of trouble this sudden event might cause for jockeys.

The field for the Tote-Portland Handicap, the 3.40 race at Doncaster on Wednesday 13 September, was at full speed, just over halfway in the extended 5-furlong sprint. *Madraco*, a 14–1 shot ridden by Paul Cook, was leading a group of horses and going well when there was a loud crack from the horse's vicinity. *Madraco* had broken a hind leg.

The horse collapsed, and Paul Cook was thrown out of the saddle. *Pendor Dancer*, ridden by Ian Johnson, crashed into the fallen horse. Ray Cochrane, on *Tolo*, did his best to take his horse over the two fallers, but he too came down.

Cochrane was soon on his feet, nursing a broken left collar-bone, but the other two jockeys lay very still until the ambulances arrived 10 minutes later. Cook had a fractured right foot, a broken right thumb, a broken collar-bone and broken ribs. Johnson had back pain, later diagnosed as a broken bone in his back. The injured *Madraco*, a horse owned by Bernard Hampson, was taken to the Equine Research Station at Newmarket for surgery.

The race was won by *Craft Express* (25–1) with *Farmer Jack* (40–1) second and *Gallant Hope* (14–1) third.

The cause of the serious accident was initially a mystery, although people from all quarters had their theories. The Clerk of the Course inspected the course and passed it fit for racing. Two days later, however, the mystery disappeared.

In the first race on Friday 15 September, the Laurent Perrier Rosé Champagne Stakes, *Able Player*, ridden by Billy Newnes and looking good for a surprise at 50–1, fell suddenly between the 2- and 3-furlong marks. Fortunately, the horse was unhurt and Newnes suffered only bruising.

When the course was inspected again, it was clear that there were holes in the track that weren't caused by the accidents. Subsidence in the drainage system was blamed, the race meeting was abandoned, and the St Leger transferred to a safer course at Ayr.

FAMOUS LAST WORDS
CHELTENHAM, MARCH 1990

The 1990 Tote Gold Cup provided a sensational climax to the Cheltenham Festival.

Before the Gold Cup, the nation's attention was heaped on *Desert Orchid*, Richard Burridge's majestic grey, variously called 'the darling of the nation', 'the shining white charger' and 'the national love object'. More often he was simply 'Dessie', already a legend and becoming an industry. You could buy Dessie books, Dessie videos, Dessie clothes, Dessie mugs, Dessie pictures and Dessie almost anything. Like *Red Rum*, it could only end in 'Now showing at your local cinema' and 'Manure for sale'.

Desert Orchid, Gold Cup winner in 1989, was 10–11 favourite to repeat his success. Trained by David Elsworth, ridden by Richard Dunwoody, *Desert Orchid* was in good form and still of darling character. His career record was 31 wins in 60 races, reaping over £480,000 in total prize money. Although Cheltenham wasn't his favourite course, *Desert Orchid* was a near certainty.

The race itself was very fast. *Desert Orchid* made much of the running, but *Ten of Spades*, ridden by Kevin Mooney, pushed him hard. At the third last, *Ten of Spades* still had the lead, *Desert Orchid* was second, but Mark Pitman was having a wonderful ride on *Toby Tobias*. Then *Ten of Spades* flagged, slipped back to fourth and fell at the second last. That left three horses with a chance – *Desert Orchid*, *Toby*

Tobias and ... check your racecards now ... the 100–1 outsider *Norton's Coin*.

Someone should have made a video showing the expressions on the faces of the 56,884 spectators. Their first gaze of disbelief came when *Desert Orchid* faded out of the running. The next came during the run-in, when 50 yards (45.7m) out, as late as he could leave it, Graham McCourt took *Norton's Coin* to the front. The 100–1 outsider held off the gallant *Toby Tobias* to win by three-quarters of a length. *Desert Orchid* was third, a further four lengths adrift. The delighted McCourt rode through to the winner's enclosure and greeted the horse's owner-trainer, Sirrell Griffiths, by throwing Griffiths's cap to the crowd and patting the balding head revealed. Griffiths did not seem to mind one jot.

In these days of big-money owners, syndicated horses and the importance of breeding, it was becoming difficult to imagine a modern-day situation comparable to *Signorinetta*'s Derby in 1908, when a small-time owner-trainer brought his 100–1 pet horse to compete in a big race and scooped the prize and the pleasure. Yet the story of *Norton's Coin* was just as dramatic.

Sirrell Griffiths, a 50-year-old dairy farmer, was the breeder and owner of *Norton's Coin*. He kept the nine-year-old chestnut gelding in the company of hens and trained the horse himself. Griffiths was permitted to train only his own horses. There were three in all.

Norton's Coin was accustomed to carrying over 15st (95.2kg) Griffiths's weight – and the trainer rode him most mornings. But other people near to Griffiths's yard, 5 miles (8km) outside Carmarthen, also had their chance to ride, whether they be Griffiths's sons or a neighbour. *Norton's Coin* was of no special pedigree. The sire and the dam cost only £1,160 between them.

Before the 1990 Tote Gold Cup, *Norton's Coin* had won four races, worth £23,000, which compared unfavourably with *Desert Orchid*'s £423,000 winnings. At 100–1 Griffiths's horse was the longest-priced winner in Gold Cup history, which stretched back to 1924. One of the biggest steeplechasing upsets of all time came about because a mix-up had caused *Norton's Coin* to miss entry dates for the Cathcart Challenge Cup and the Mildmay of Flete.

On the morning of the 1990 Tote Gold Cup a racing correspondent of one national newspaper assessed *Desert Orchid*'s forthcoming certain victory: 'Thoughts of defeat for any reason other than a freak mishap cannot be seriously entertained. That prediction may wind up in the book of famous last words, but any analysis of the race must logically be confined not so much to whether *Desert Orchid* can capture a second Gold Cup, but by how far he will win it and who will be second.'

That's the beauty of horse racing. It will never lose its potential for strangeness and it will always attract 'famous last words'.

THE GRAND NATIONAL THAT NEVER WAS

AINTREE, LIVERPOOL, APRIL 1993

Punters waged £75 million on the 1993 Grand National, and every top tipster picked a winner, but nobody was able to predict the eventual outcome. After two false starts, the race was officially declared void, even though seven horses completed the course.

Thirty-nine horses cantered to the start in good time for the 3.50p.m. race. It was important to start on time because the race was being televised around the world. Girths had been checked early and there was a bit of hanging around. Then came a protest from about 30 animal rights demonstrators and the schedules were disrupted anyway.

Police chased the protesters across the course and over the fences for several minutes before the racecourse was cleared. Meanwhile, horses and jockeys grew agitated at the start. Some people said the delay contributed to what followed. Others said it made no difference.

The horses spread 65 yards (59.4m) across the track and at 3.58p.m. the starter, Captain Brown, made his first attempt to get the race under way. He brought them up to the starting-tape but the tape caught over several riders as it was raised. The starter declared a false start and all the horses came back.

The system for declaring a false start was almost as old as the race. A flag man was stationed at the side of the course before the first fence. If the starter didn't drop his red flag then the flag man should know it was a false start. The flag man should then try to catch the jockeys' attention with his own flag.

This system proved crucially inefficient for the second false start.

The starter, using a megaphone, tried to make himself heard over the noise of the nearby crowd. The horses came to a sagging tape. In fact *Formula One*, near the outside, came so close to the tape that he had his head over it. When the starter raised the tape it caught under *Formula One*'s head and wrapped itself around the next jockey, Richard Dunwoody, who was almost strangled. Dunwoody immediately knew that it had to be a false start. He wasn't going anywhere and his horse, the aptly named *Won't Be Gone Long*, certainly wasn't.

Nine runners and riders were left near the start. The rest set off at a typically fast gallop towards the first fence. The starter's red flag failed to unfurl and the flag man failed to make any impression on the horses on the inside.

As the horses continued on the first circuit, trainers and stable-lads tried to signal the jockeys to stop. Some jockeys realised what was happening and pulled up their mounts. *Travel Over* was pulled up lame anyway, after setting off with the tape knotted around his legs. Others fell at fences. Fortunately none of the horses or jockeys were badly injured.

John White, on *Esha Ness*, had seen the flag man on the first false-start but not on the second. White was in a pack of half a dozen riders at the front of the 'race'. When he reached The Chair he saw a cone and a red flag and people waving to him. White assumed these were animal rights protesters rather than course officials. He did his best to ignore them and get on with the job of riding a Grand National winner. There were horses all around him and it seemed like the race was still on. White was focusing solely on the race, concentrating despite the rain on his goggles, the noise of the strong wind and the sounds of the nearby horses.

White road brilliantly on *Esha Ness* – all the way to the finishing-post. His victory celebrations were very natural. It was clear to everyone around that White felt that he had won the Grand National. And then Dean Gallagher shouted across those depressing words: 'It was no race.'

At 4.40p.m. the race was declared void.

The starter left the course under a police escort.

The eventual enquiry blamed the outdated starting system and inadequate recall system and concluded that the flag man had failed to do his job. No disciplinary action was taken against the race officials but senior racecourse officials began to study new recommendations for clearer pre-start assembly-points and radio links between starter and recall-man.

It was one of a spate of races that ended in chaos that year. Richard Dunwoody completed an extra circuit on *Mighty Mogul* at Haydock Park, a race at Wolverhampton had been declared void, and then the Queen's Head Novices' Chase at Kelso was declared void after a veterinary surgeon sent jockeys round one fence.

SEVEN OUT OF SEVEN
ASCOT, SEPTEMBER 1996

In the 2 o'clock race at Ascot, on Saturday 28 September 1996, Sardinian-born jockey Lanfranco 'Frankie' Dettori rode the 2–1 favourite *Wall Street* in a field of seven. Wall Street made all the running and won by half a length in a tight finish.

In the 2.35, a 6-furlong sprint, Dettori went with a 12–1 shot called *Diffident*. He held off the 15–8 favourite, *Lucayan Prince*, and ten other horses to win by a short head.

Dettori's mount in the 3.20, *Mark of Esteem* at 100–30, was coaxed through a narrow gap for a late run to the finishing-post. The horse won by one and a quarter lengths. Seven ran.

The 3.55 race had 26 runners and Dettori rode *Decorated Hero* at 7–1. The horse, the top weight, came home easily by 3½ lengths. Four out of four for Dettori.

With three races left on the card, bookmakers were very worried. They realised that Dettori was on top form and had three more possible winners. There were even punters who had gone with Dettori for the whole card.

The 4.30 went to *Fatefully*, the 7–4 favourite, who won by a neck in a field of 18 runners. The winning jockey was Frankie Dettori.

The 5 o'clock had five runners. The 5–4 joint favourite, *Lochangel*, won easily by three-quarters of a length. It was Dettori's sixth of the day.

That left the 5.35 race with 18 runners. The odds on Dettori's mount, *Fujiyama Crest*, shortened dramatically from 12–1 to 2–1 favourite. Bookmakers were laying off money where they could, but most of them couldn't. Everyone was too wise. Something sensational was in the air. Nothing like this had been seen since Gordon Richards had ridden 12 consecutive winners in 1933. But Richards did it over three days. No none had ever won every race on a card.

Dettori rode the 5.35 from the front and won by a neck. He returned to the enclosure joyously and dismounted with one of his trademark flying-ejector leaps which he reserved for special occasions. It was indeed one of horse racing's greatest-ever achievements. An editorial in *The Times* described it as 'the equivalent of a racing driver winning every race in the Grand Prix, a bowler taking ten wickets in an innings of a Test match and then making a century, or a golfer scoring straight birdies in the final round of the Open, ending with a hole in one at the eighteenth.'

Dettori's seven wins from seven races completed a very bad day for bookmakers and a great day for punters, including a 30-year-old man from Morecambe, Lancashire, who won £500,000 from a £64 accumulator bet.

A few days later, Terry Harper of Trowbridge, Wiltshire, wrote to *The Times* to say that, as a bet on four selections in four races is known as a Yankee, perhaps a bet on seven selections in seven races should become a Frankie.

WHEN THE GRAND NATIONAL WAS RUN ON A MONDAY

AINTREE, LIVERPOOL, APRIL 1997

At 2.45p.m. the Aintree atmosphere was buzzing. Hospitality suites were bubbling, bookmakers were shouting the odds, and 70,000 people were waiting excitedly for the big race.

An hour later, when the 150th Grand National was scheduled to start, the racecourse was virtually empty.

The afternoon was changed by two phone calls. The first, at 2.49p.m., to Fazakerley Hospital, warned that a bomb planted in the racecourse car-park would detonate at 3.50p.m. Three minutes later, at 2.52p.m., Marsh Lane Police Station, Bootle, received a similar phone call. The warnings had to be taken seriously because they contained a special code used by the Irish Republican Army (IRA), the same code that had been used before the 1996 Docklands lorry bomb.

A few minutes after the second phone call, 30 policemen walked towards the Aintree parade ring. They stationed themselves on the perimeter of the ring, 20ft (6.1m) apart. The senior police officer summoned the head parade steward. An announcement came over the tannoy: 'Please move away from the parade ring towards the stand area.'

'That was the moment when, for the first time ever at Aintree, the crowd, not the horses, came under starters' orders,' said Angela Candlin in the *Liverpool Echo*.

The parade ring emptied and people strolled across to the stands. They stayed for ten minutes. Then another tannoy announcement asked them to move on to the course itself. The final instruction was for them to clear the racecourse via the Seeds Lane exit.

They walked the course. The pace was much slower than usual between the jumps. They crossed the Melling Road. They walked in droves, calm and good-humoured, with no idea why they were leaving. A group of lads sang 'You'll never walk alone'. There were a few fallers at the perimeter fences but no serious casualties. And then the racecourse was empty except for police and bomb-disposal experts who had the task of checking the 7,000 cars in the racecourse car-park.

The racegoers – now raceleavers – hung around in the vicinity, expecting to be called back at any time. After two or three hours, however, they realised that the race would not be run that day. Meanwhile, the standard sports-event segregation was breaking down. Lords and commoners mixed together: waiters and waitresses dressed in shirt-sleeves and carrying tea towels; jockeys still wearing their coloured silks; a well-dressed lady in a fish-and-chip shop asking, in a public-school voice, 'What exactly is a fritter?'

An estimated 40,000 of the evacuated crowd came from outside the immediate Merseyside area. Over half of these were dependent upon their stranded cars. Local people did their utmost to help them. A woman holding a tea-party invited in passers-by until she was entertaining a hundred. Another woman served tea in shifts of ten.

People spoke later of a 'wartime spirit'. Ten emergency centres were set up: volunteers made tea and coffee; local supermarkets and grocers contributed food; and prisoners at Walton Jail made 500 sandwiches. Local radio presenters helped to coordinate offers of help. Car-drivers stopped to pick up hitchhikers on motorway sliproads. A hundred agitated horses, left at the racecourse, were tended by one stable-lad, Phil Sharp, who had defied police instructions and stayed behind. The horses were finally led away four hours after the initial evacuation.

Then, as time went on, makeshift accommodation was provided for 20,000 people. There were 55 beds at Maghull High School, 54 at Litherland High School and 18 at Litherland Moss Primary School. Church halls were offered for sleeping, and 15 sports and leisure centres displayed vacancy signs for blanket-and-breakfast. Everton Sports Centre took 500 people. Staff at the Adelphi Hotel arranged mattresses and camp-beds in every available space. Some strays made their own bivouac arrangements at the side of Liverpool docks. One man slept in a hotel bath.

The racecourse car-park was reopened at 2.45p.m. the next day. The racegoers returned in their thousands to collect their cars. Meanwhile, race officials decided that the race would go ahead at 5p.m. on the Monday. No private cars were allowed on the racecourse and every spectator was frisked on entry. The police received a further bomb warning but they allowed the race to be run. A surprisingly large crowd of 20,000 turned up, and everything passed off smoothly. Prime Minister John Major and Princess Anne attended the event.

The race was comfortably won by *Lord Gyllene*, who made all the running and romped home by 25 lengths. The winning trainer was Steve Brookshaw and the 24-year-old jockey, Tony Dobbin, was ironically from Northern Ireland. The horse was owned by multi-millionaire Stan Clarke. I can claim a small personal connection with Mr Clarke. Eight months after the Grand National, he bought my late parents' cottage and added it to his Staffordshire estate next door. It's the only time I have ever sold a house to the owner of a current Grand National winner after the race had been won on a Monday.

BEN JOHNSON, TWO HORSES AND A STOCK CAR

PRINCE EDWARD ISLAND, CANADA, OCTOBER 1998

The Interspecies Olympics gained a new event when the fastest sprinter in the world took on two horses and a stock car.

The venue was Charlottetown Driving Park on a stormy evening full of heavy rain and a strong north-easterly wind. Over 5,000 spectators packed into the arena to watch a full card of harness-racing and one strange race – Ben Johnson against two horses and a machine.

Ben Johnson was still the fastest man in the world. At the 1988 Seoul Olympics, he had run the 100 metres in 9.79 seconds only to test positively for a steroid drug called stanozolol. Johnson was suspended for two years, and stripped of the gold medal. His world record was expunged.

After failing another drug test, in 1993, Johnson was banned for life by the International Amateur Athletics Federation, and the Canadian courts upheld the judgment five years later. In 1998, Ben Johnson's last chance of continuing his athletics career seemed to have gone. He was now 36 years old but still believed he could compete at the highest level. He certainly thought he could beat two horses and a stock car under the conditions set by the handicapper.

Ben Johnson, the fastest man in the world, would sprint 80 metres. It was his first competitive race for five years.

Fast 'n Flashy, a fast-stepping harness-racing horse, would trot 100 metres with Wally Hennessey holding the reins.

Windsong, a 17-year-old thoroughbred workhorse, would gallop 120 metres. It would be the horse's first ever race. *Windsong* would be ridden by Lloyd Duffy, an experienced local jockey.

The stock car, driven by Mike Ryan, would travel 140 metres. 'On your marks!'

'Under orders!'

'Start your engines!'

Windsong was unfamiliar with the loud tannoy and flashing cameras, and looked very nervous before the race. When the stock-car engine roared into life, Windsong was spooked. The horse set off with a suspiciously false start. Then they were all away.

The spectators roared at the spectacle of four very different running styles. Ben Johnson was running at full speed, and *Fast 'n Flashy* was away and trotting. But the stock car slewed across the muddy track with wheels spinning.

Despite lacking shoes, *Windsong* ran well on the muddy ground. The thoroughbred overtook Ben Johnson to win in a time of seven seconds, and the trotter caught Johnson just before the finishing line. Ben Johnson was third, several metres behind the winner.

Maybe George Orwell's *Animal Farm* maxim was correct after all – *Four legs good, two legs bad.*

While some people thought the Charlottetown race was ridiculous, others pointed out that many television programmes were even more ridiculous. Indeed, Ben Johnson had already turned down a television company's offer for him to race against a cheetah. Johnson ran the Charlottetown race for free. The beneficiary was the Children's Wish Foundation, a charity helping children with life-threatening diseases.

A RACEHORSE IN THE DOGHOUSE

KEMPTON PARK, JUNE 2004

A six-year-old gelding called *Tiny Tim* raced against a black greyhound called *Simply Fabulous* in an attempt to settle the long-running debate about which species was the faster. It was a 2-furlong race, the first on a Kempton Park evening racecard, and interested onlookers sharpened their wit on the novelty of the occasion.

'I think *Simply Fabulous* is the underdog.' 'He's the only dog.'

'Who's riding *Tiny Tim*?'

'Fergus Sweeney.'

'Who's on the dog?'

'No one.'

'Should make the weight.'

The betting was a serious matter, and punters deliberated long and hard about cross-species comparisons. The 2-furlong distance was more familiar to a greyhound than a racehorse, and this particular greyhound had won 14 of his 35 races. But eight-year-old *Simply Fabulous* was now an old dog – retired from racing for 18 months – and this was a new trick.

In contrast, *Tiny Tim* was an in-form racehorse with a win at Brighton and two seconds in the past month. The bay gelding had been placed in all but two of his previous ten starts. But the horse was accustomed to much longer distances than 2 furlongs.

The horse was on familiar ground. The greyhound would be unaccustomed to running on grass, and the dry weather was expected to be a further advantage to the horse. Other people pointed out that racehorses reacted badly to nearby dogs, but *Tiny Tim*'s trainer, Andrew Balding, opted for blinkers so that his horse wouldn't be put off by a greyhound running alongside.

The money favoured the horse. At the time of the race, 5.50, *Tiny Tim* was 13–8 on favourite, and *Simply Fabulous* was 6–5.

It was a one-horse race but the horse came second. First, *Simply Fabulous*. Second, *Tiny Tim*. Two ran.

The official distance was seven lengths. That is, seven *horse* lengths, the equivalent of 15 dog lengths.

The greyhound's winning time was 23.29 seconds, and the horse completed the course in 24.63 seconds. The losing jockey, Fergus Sweeney, was disappointed and a little surprised. He knew that the short distance had been critical and felt the horse would have won over an extra furlong. Sweeney was looking forward to a rematch.

Meanwhile, David Hood, the owner of *Simply Fabulous*, claimed that his dog's success must have been partly down to the pre-race preparation. He had fed *Simply Fabulous* bangers and mash – the dog's favourite meal.

Of course the matter of the faster species was still not settled. It depended on the horse, the dog, the track, the distance and the day.

MAN BEATS HORSE
LLANWRTYD WELLS, WALES, JUNE 2004

It all started with a conversation in the Neuadd Arms Hotel in the late 1970s. Gordon Green, then the landlord, heard some local customers debating the familiar man vs horse question.

'Over a distance,' one man said. 'It has to be over a distance.' According to Welsh legend, Guto Nyth-Bran beat a horse in an eighteenth-century race across Cardigan and then never rose again after his back was slapped so much during the celebrations.

Could it be done again – without the back-slapping? Gordon Green turned pub talk into action by launching the annual Man vs Horse Marathon in 1980. The prize money for the first man to beat all the horses over 22 miles (35.4km) grew from year to year without being won. Then, in 2004, in the race's silver jubilee year, 27-year-old Huw Lobb became the first human to win. His prize was £25,000.

The gap between first horse and first human was large at first – 43 minutes in 1980 – but it varied substantially from year to year. As the course was adapted to provide a more equal contest, more and more experienced runners took an interest, and a serious challenge became possible. In 2000 Mark Croasdale finished less than two minutes behind the winning horse and rider. Croasdale might have done well the following year but for a couple of wrong turns.

In 2004, the race began in the customary place – outside the Neuadd Arms Hotel in the centre of the town. Runners and riders gathered on the second Saturday in June. There were individuals prepared to run the full 22 miles and three-person relay teams who could share the load. (Relay teams had first beaten the leading horse in 1985. Four years later a mountain-biker, Tim Gould, beat the first horse by nearly three minutes, but mountain-bikes were excluded from 1994 because an anomaly in the Road Traffic Act banned them from racing on bridleways.)

The 2004 race was marked by the unveiling of a permanent memorial to Screaming Lord Sutch who had been the race's official starter for the eleven years before his death (only a few days after the 1999 race). Lord Sutch, a former rock star, had stood for Parliament on 39 occasions, most notably as a candidate for the Monster Raving Loony Party campaigning with the slogan 'Vote for Insanity – you know it makes sense'.

The race was started by Cynthia Payne, author of *An English Madam*. The horses and humans had staggered starting-times, 15 minutes apart, in order to make the race safer. A record 566 athletes took part in the race, and 47 horses and riders. Once out in the open country, they faced a gruelling course – along roads, up and down hills, in and out of streams and rivers, across open moorland and down farm tracks. The runners and riders have to avoid each other. A runaway horse can be very dangerous.

Earlier that year Huw Lobb had run the London Marathon and finished as the fourth fastest Briton. Now he covered the 22 miles in two hours, five minutes and 19 seconds. His time was two minutes and 17 seconds faster than Zoe White on her horse *Kay Bee Jay*. Lobb won at odds of 16–1 and told one interviewer that he would spend some of his prize money on a better pair of running shoes.

Llanwrtyd Wells has earned a reputation for strange events. Besides the Man vs Horse Marathon the small town stages the World Bog Snorkelling Competition and the Gourmet Food Festival. Where will it end? Maybe one day we shall see the Animal Olympics.

SEAGULLS IN THE HOME STRAIGHT

MELBOURNE, AUSTRALIA, MARCH 2005

During the last race of the day at Sandown, home of Australia's Melbourne Racing Club, a huge number of seagulls settled on the course in the home straight. Seagulls on the course had been a long-standing problem – or even a long-perching one – but this flock of birds created a particularly dangerous scenario.

At 5.20p.m., in fading light, 11 runners set off in the 1,200m (1,312 yard) Goldenway Handicap. The horses were about 200m (219 yards) from the finish when hundreds of birds suddenly took to the air. Every horse in the race was affected by the white and grey haze, and the riders and horses took a real buffeting.

The birds caused five horses to fall. *Chop Chop*'s rider Brady Cross was taken to hospital with a suspected broken left arm and other casualties included Luke Nolan (sprained thumb) on *Miss Ab Fab*, Chris Symons (bruised shoulder) on *Aussie Loti* and apprentice jockey Michael Guthrie (bruised and shaken) on *Shove Over*.

Diamond Hailey's jockey, Darren Gauci, suffered a ricked neck and chipped teeth. Gauci had been given his ride shortly before the start and he must have been wishing he had passed it up. He was well back in the field, going steadily, when he ran into the birds, and the horses in front of him suddenly turned into black dots. Gauci had no idea he was falling from his horse until he hit the ground.

When Peter Mertens was hit by the birds his horse *Elmatilla* turned through 90 degrees and went sideways towards the car-park. Mertens somehow managed to change direction to straight ahead and he did remarkably well to cross the line first, especially as he had four seagulls sitting on his lap. Matt Laurie, the trainer of *Elmatilla*, thought he had the first winner of his career, but the race was later declared void.

American Graffiti was second past the finishing-post and *Bella Corona*, the favourite, was third. Nicholas Ryan, on *Bella Corona*, did magnificently just to stay in the saddle.

WHAT'S IN A NAME?
OCEANPORT, NEW JERSEY, USA, AUGUST 2010

Track announcer Larry Collmus knew he had to be careful with the names of two horses in the seventh race at Monmouth Park. 'Don't mess up,' he told himself when he saw that the ten runners included *My Wife Knows Everything* and *The Wife Doesn't Know*.

Collmus's research was invaluable when it came to an exciting run-in: 'Into the final furlong,' Collmus announced, '*My Wife Knows Everything, The Wife Doesn't Know.* They are one and two. Of course they are. *My Wife Knows Everything* in front, to the outside, *The Wife Doesn't Know. My Wife Knows Everything, The Wife Doesn't Know. My Wife Knows Everything* more than *The Wife Doesn't Know.*'

When the two horses passed the finishing-post Larry Collmus let out a sigh of relief.

Horse names are allowed a maximum of 18 characters so the names of the two horses had been registered slightly differently. *My Wife Knows Everything* was submitted as 'Mywifenosevrything' and *The Wife Doesn't Know* was down as 'Thewifedoesntknow'.

Strange horse names could fill another book. They have to be unique to satisfy the horse racing authorities. Names shouldn't have figures, hyphens, full stops, commas, arithmetic signs or exclamation marks, and they should be no more than seven syllables. It has to be a new name (unless the statutes on the name have run out) and not one that is 'suggestive or has a vulgar, obscene or insulting meaning'. Occasionally, however, a name will slip past the censors. Examples include *Hoof Hearted*, *Who Gives a Donald*, *Peony's Envy*, *Noble Locks*, *WearTheFoxHat* and *Geespot*.

Owners can name a horse after a famous person but only if they have the person's permission. Book and movie titles are not allowed, and the horse's name mustn't have commercial significance unless either permission has been received or the name has an alternative meaning that is in common usage. Nearly 500,000 names are in active use in the USA and about 250,000 in the United Kingdom.

About 3,000 famous horse names have been delisted because the horse was so brilliant that it would be unfair to give a lesser horse the same name. Examples include *Frankel*, *Arkle*, *Shergar* and *Red Rum*, all of whom will be still famous when the normal statutes on names run out.

My own favourite horse names include *Fifty Shades of Hay*, *A Horse called Man*, *Another Horse* and *Neigh Chance*. But *Neigh Chance* failed to live up to its name when it won a race at Sandown Park in 2009.

HORSES ELECTROCUTED IN THE PADDOCK

NEWBURY, BERKSHIRE, FEBRUARY 2011

It was lovely weather at Newbury and a good day for racing. In the paddock, before the first race of the day, the former champion jockey Graham Thorner exchanged greetings with *Marching Song*, a horse he co-owned. Then, while walking round the paddock, *Marching Song* suddenly collapsed and died. The horse had run eight previous races with no sign of any medical condition.

Another horse, *Fenix Two*, also fell and died in the paddock, and other horses showed signs of distress. *Kid Cassidy* was withdrawn after stumbling and *The Merry Giant* seemed out of sorts.

These horses were among the ten entrants for a Novice Hurdle, the first of seven races on the card that Saturday. The two deaths happened within 30 seconds of the horses showing discomfort. Veterinary surgeons and stable hands could feel tingling sensations while they examined the horses. They were getting mild shocks off the grass or the animals.

The hearts of the running horses were checked before the start of the race and runners went to the start. *The Merry Giant* ran the race but finished last. The horse was clearly traumatised.

There was a 9,000 crowd at Newbury that Saturday but the day's racing was abandoned after the first race. The last six races on the card were non-starters.

The British Horse Racing Authority, Southern Electric Power Distribution and the police conducted an investigation into the tragedy. The eventual report described the deaths as 'accidental electrocution'. Medically, the cause of the two deaths was sudden cardiac arrest.

Those horses wearing metal horseshoes seemed more affected than those with aluminium horseshoes. Quadrupeds are more susceptible than bipeds because the electrical charge can flow through one set of a horse's legs and then course through the horse's body. Human beings were better protected, especially if they were wearing leather-soled shoes, plastic-soled shoes or rubber Wellington boots. Electrical charges take the path of least resistance.

The tragedy was seen as an unusual one-off accident. According to an article in the *Daily Express*, a cable laid 42 years previously had been disturbed by workers digging just before the Newbury race meeting. Wet ground conditions and the horses' vulnerability to electricity also contributed to the deaths and injuries. After the report an electricity cable running beneath the parade ring was removed. It had been leaking electricity. Racing at Newbury resumed six days after the incident in the paddock.

REMOUNTING NOT PERMITTED

TOWCESTER, MARCH 2011

A recent rule change stipulated that jockeys could no longer remount during races after they had fallen or been unseated. Previously there had been some farcical races where jockeys had run around the course attempting to catch their horses and remount.

The rule was brought in to ensure that horses didn't aggravate injuries. In 2005, a top-class horse called *Kauto Star* had missed a lot of the season after the horse's jockey had remounted and continued a race without realising that the horse was injured. The new rule did not apply if a jockey fell or was unseated on the way to the start of a race, but an attending doctor had to confirm the jockey was still fit to participate, and a veterinary surgeon had to check the horse's health.

The rule seemed to make sense – jockeys had to stay in the saddle to complete a race – but it created other problems, such as the increased possibility of void races. One of the first instances of the law change came at Towcester on 17 March 2011, when all four horses failed to finish in the 4.25 race. The race was declared void. The jockeys knew that remounting their horse would cause a disqualification.

Two horses fell early in the race – *Zhukov* brought down *Cengiz* – but the other two runners continued the race. Coming to the second last Adrian Lane on *Identity Parade* was leading by four or five lengths but the horse refused the fence and threw his jockey. Peter Toole on *Radharc Na Mara* looked likely to win the race but he was unseated while trying to avoid *Identity Parade*.

Tom Dreaper, the trainer of *Radharc Na Mara*, was disappointed. His horse was fine and could have been remounted to win the prize money. In Ireland there was no such rule banning remounting.

There are of course many other reasons for a void race. They have included malfunctioning stalls, flag failures (e.g. use of the wrong flag), spectator interference, horses taking the wrong course, earthquakes, bad weather (e.g. fog) and so on. Sometimes jockeys don't see the yellow flag (stopping the race) or the chequered flag warning of a hazard.

A WILD HORSE RACE

CHEYENNE, WYOMING, USA, JULY 2013

Contestants say that it is dangerous, explosive and exciting, but animal rights activists say that it is a cruel sport which upsets the animals. The event in question is the wild horse race, where unbroken horses are let out of a chute and teams of three compete to be the first to tame and mount the horse and ride it past the judges' box. This is different to horse racing as most people know it.

Wild horse racing began in the late 1890s as one of the original rodeo events. It was included at the first Cheyenne Frontier Days rodeo in 1896 and even in the 1930s wild horse races had a Wild West atmosphere. Subsequently their popularity began to fade, reaching a low point in the 1960s and early 1970s. In 1973 there were 592 sanctioned rodeos in the USA but only 13 had wild horse races and cowboys had lost interest in the sport. That year, however, a meeting of 53 cowboys in a barn eventually led to the formation of the Professional Wild Horse Racers Association.

In the late 1970s a 28-page rule book was established for the event. Cowboys had to be at least 19 years of age to take part, competitors weren't allowed to saddle a horse while the animal was lying down, and only one member of the team could report to the judge. When a horse was mounted the lead shank had to be let go after three full jumps by the horse or steps in any direction. Competitors had to wear a cowboy hat (which usually fell off) and they could be disqualified for arguing with a judge.

The rule book also provided guidelines on how to touch a horse, but over the years some people haven't felt that that is good enough. According to one report, in the 1990s, the RSPCA telephoned Mount Isa Rotary Rodeo Inc. in Australia and threatened a court case unless the wild horse race was cut from the rodeo.

In July 2013 a reporter from the *Northern Wyoming Daily News* described the wild horse race exploits of a team called the Banquet Boys. First, competing teams drew lots for which horse they would try to tame. Then the three people in the team – Matt Duncan (the shank man), James Kircher (the mugger) and James Harmon (the rider) – readied themselves for action. On the release of a brown horse with a black mane the shank man held on to a rope (maximum length 16ft/4.9m) tied to the horse's bridge, and then he attempted to control the animal. Meanwhile the mugger tried to hold the horse's head using a halter, perhaps even twisting the horse's ear and wrestling the neck to keep the horse occupied, while the rider tried to saddle the horse. Some muggers tried to calm the horse by singing in its ear. All this happens in a noisy background with an announcer talking on the tannoy, spectators and competitors shouting and cannons being fired. The horses could be spooked.

When the horse was saddled and secured the rider mounted and set off on a part circuit of the ring to reach the judges' station. Then the other two members of the team jumped over the fence that separated the track from observation area. It was necessary to seek a safe area because wild horses were sometimes running dangerously loose in the arena, having thrown the rider or slipped the shank man and mugger. As between six and 15 teams could be competing in the same arena it was not uncommon for the humans to suffer broken legs, fractured skulls or broken wrists. 'It's not whether you're going to get hurt, but when,' one experienced competitor said.

To win a contest the horse usually has to be tamed and ridden to the finish within 30 or 40 seconds of the start, and the rider must pass the finishing point while still sitting in the saddle. A team is not allowed to win a race if a horse has been injured.

The Banquet Boys had taken a minute but were within seconds of reaching the finish when their horse suddenly stopped and Harmon, the rider, was stumped. Time expired before the Banquet Boys could coax the horse past the finishing line.

OVER 99 LENGTHS BEHIND SECOND PLACE

WORCESTER, OCTOBER 2013

Andrew Thornton was a 40-year-old jump jockey with nearly 23 years of National Hunt experience when he rode *Spike Mac* in the Ladbrokes Maiden Hurdle at Worcester. His winning rides had included the 1998 Cheltenham Gold Cup on *Cool Dawn*, but his career catalogue of setbacks included a broken leg (two months after the Gold Cup win), five collar-bone fractures and a broken left ankle.

Spike Mac, one of four runners, soon lived up to his 50–1 odds by trailing the third-place horse by 2 furlongs. Then the odds-on favourite *Court Appeal*, pressed by *Bob Tucker*, fell at the third last hurdle. That left A.P. McCoy, on *Bob Tucker*, with a long lead, only needing to jump the last two hurdles to win, which he duly did. Miss L. Brooke on *Mr Bachster* eased up on the run-in as she had no chance of winning.

Thornton, on *Spike Mac*, was so far behind that he hadn't realised *Court Appeal* had fallen. A flag man waved Thornton down and explained that the Clerk of the Course was arranging a marker that would allow the jockey to bypass the hurdle with the fallen horse. *Court Appeal* had been winded in the fall and was on the ground on the other side of the hurdle.

The discussion between Thornton and the flag man went on for 30 or 40 seconds before Thornton was convinced that there would be no penalty if he missed the next flight.

By then the other two horses were well out of sight. But the third-place prize money – around £400 – was still there for the taking.

'My horse was as slow as a hearse,' Thornton told *Racing Post* later. 'And I was so far behind that the Clerk of the Course, who was stood with the stewards' secretary, radioed down to the guys at the hurdle to stop me jumping it because there was a horse prostrate on the ground.'

Thornton went on to jump the last two flights and finish third. The distances were 25 lengths and over 99 lengths.

HORSE vs BICYCLE

LEOPARDSTOWN, IRELAND, AUGUST 2014 AND ALBERTA, CANADA, OCTOBER 2014

Races between horses and cyclists are as old as the bicycle. When the bike was popularised, at the beginning of the twentieth century, a writer in *The Velocipede* magazine said that 'walking was on its last legs'. Since then all sorts of bicycle transport have been used – two-wheelers, tricycles, unicycles, mountain bikes, recumbent bikes and so on.

In the 1880s and 1890s the great showman William Cody, known as 'Buffalo Bill', challenged bicyclists to races. Buffalo Bill set stiff rules. In a race in Milan he was allowed to use ten horses in three hours while his opponent, Romulus Buni, cycled all the way. At the end of the three hours Buni had covered 61½ miles (99km) and Buffalo Bill 63¾ miles (102.7km).

Bicycle vs horse races have taken place more recently. In August 2014, in the middle of the flat-racing season, jockey Pat Smullen, 37, was well on his way to becoming Irish Champion Jockey for the seventh time. Smullen took a few minutes out of his usual racetrack mission and competed against a top Irish cyclist, 30-year-old Nicolas Roche, who had achieved numerous top-ten finishes in Grand Tour stages.

The two men raced each other on adjacent tracks. Smullen was riding *Moonbi Creek* over 2 furlongs on the grassy racecourse while Roche cycled 437 yards (400m) on a smooth-surfaced road.

The commentator was Des Scahill, a veteran of the airwaves, famous for describing many exciting run-ins, including *Dawn Run*'s last-stride win in the 1986 Cheltenham Gold Cup. Scahill was just the man for the showdown between horse and bicycle but he had to deal with the possibility of a false start. 'Pat Smullen has gone very early,' said Scahill. 'Nicholas has got a big task on his hands, he's coming up the tarmac here, he's cycling for his life towards the elbow.'

Horse and bicycle zoomed along at over 30mph (48.3km/h). At the halfway stage the horse had a lead of a couple of lengths but the space between the two riders grew, and Pat Smullen on *Moonbi Creek* came home a comfortable winner. The participants – jockey, horse, cyclist, bike – made their way to the winners' enclosure for a presentation. The race raised funds for the Children's Medical and Research Foundation at Our Lady's Hospital in Crumlin.

Two months later, in October 2014, a different kind of 'horse vs bicycle' race took place in Alberta, Canada. Monika Smith was riding her mare *Sheba* on the Elbow Falls trail in Kananaskis Country. She had come prepared for a 30-mile (48.3km) endurance ride with stethoscope, sponge, water-treatment equipment, matches, flare, lunch, horse biscuits, plastic bag, jacket, halter and shank, hoof pick and lots more.

It was a fine summer's day and along the way she met a very fit cyclist who was riding a state-of-the-art mountain bike. The cyclist helped her to negotiate a gate and then rode away. The race had begun.

Monika Smith knew the trails well but she had to take care when going downhill whereas the cyclist could fly down the hills in no time. When the cyclist stopped for a break she passed him again. But she was held up on busier parts of the trail, where she had to be careful around hikers, dogwalkers and branches.

When she got to the end of the trail the cyclist was already cleaning his bike in the creek. Monika Smith took her horse into the water and gave the mare a wash.

'I didn't realise a horse could go that fast,' the mountain bike man said.

'I didn't think a human could,' said the horse rider.

The outcome of 'bicycle vs horse' races depends a lot on the type of bicycle, the horse's pedigree, the capabilities of the riders, and the terrain. Modern recumbent bikes can reach 80mph (129km/h), and that would produce a certain victory on a smooth track against the racehorse's maximum of 55mph (88.5km/h). Racing cycles might manage 40mph (64.4km/h) and road bikes 30mph (48.3km/h). But 'horse vs bicycle' will depend on the conditions and whether replacement horses are allowed over longer distances.

Shall we call it a draw?

THE PANTOMIME HORSE DERBY

GREENWICH, LONDON, DECEMBER 2014

This was the fifth year of a comedy race full of fun. Over 40 pantomime horses participated and that meant more than 80 people racing. Each horse had one person at the front of the horse and one at the rear end. The course was a quarter of a mile (400m).

The rear-end runners, bent over at 90 degrees, couldn't see a thing and had to trust their partners, and it could be sweaty inside a pantomime horse. It took some practice for the runners to achieve some rhythm whereby the person at the rear of the horse could match the stride of the person at the front, and going in the same direction helped a lot. Preparation for the race had included running on a treadmill with a horse's head on, wearing horse trousers around the house and drinking gin and tonics. Even though the course was only a quarter of a mile it included a stop for drinks so that the horses could dash into a pub and drink at both ends.

The fifth annual Greenwich race, in 2014, had a science-fiction theme, so there were appearances from Darth Vader, R2D2, Princess Leia, Queen Amidala and other legendary fictional characters. Some pairs dressed as pantomime zebras and pantomime cows. It was an opportunity for the British to demonstrate their eccentricity. Similar events have included the Thomas Vale Pantomime Horse Grand National in Birmingham and the Royal Sun Pantomime

Horse Derby, which began in 2008 for Breast Cancer Campaign.

In the league of strange competitions and eccentric behaviours, pantomime horse races rate alongside Holmfirth's welly-wanging competition, Ramsbottom's black pudding tossing and throwing the besom at the Helmsdale Highland Games. Wife-carrying competitions have become very popular – the world championships are held in Finland – and one such event took place at Hereford racecourse.

Horses, greyhounds and pigeons top the league for racing entertainment but competitions can involve other creatures. People have turned up to see ferret-racing at Stourbridge, pig-racing at Lincoln, camel-racing in Dorset and sheep-racing in Northumberland. One sheep race saw entrants called *Lady Baa Baa*, *Maadonna* and *Shearer*.

The football mascots race, which began around 2000, is in a similar league to pantomime horse racing. Many different types of animal have been depicted, although most were two-legged. The main link with horse racing was that some such races took place on actual racecourses, such as Kempton Park, albeit with low barriers. The roots of the mascots' race come from the professional mascots who appeared every week at football clubs, livening up the atmosphere for fans, looking amusing and celebrating with the crowd. But the increase in private-company mascots caused a schism and one year the event was boycotted. Some football mascots felt it was better to take part in local events rather than national ones.

SELECTED BIBLIOGRAPHY

Black, Robert, *Horse Racing in England*, 1893

Bland, Ernest (editor), *Flat Racing since 1900*, 1950

Buckingham, John, *Tales from the Weighing Room*, 1987

Champion, Bob and Jonathan Powell, *Champion's Story*, 1982

Cook, Sir Theodore, *A History of the English Turf*, 1901

Cranham, Gerry, *The Guinness Guide to Steeplechasing*, 1979

Cuming, E.D. (editor), *Squire Osbaldston, His Autobiography*, 1926

Curzon, Louis Henry, *A Mirror of the Turf*, 1892

Custance, Henry, *Riding Recollections and Turf Stories*, 1894

Day, William, *William Day's Reminiscences of the Turf*, 1886

Dighton, Adair, *My Sporting Life*, 1934

Donoghue, Steve, *Just My Story*, 1925

Donoghue, Steve, *Donoghue Up*, 1938

Ellerington, Alison, *The Kiplingcotes Derby*, 1990

Fairfax-Blakeborough, John, *The Analysis of the Turf*, 1927

Fairfax-Blakeborough, John, *Turf Who's Who*, 1932

Fairfax-Blakeborough, John, *Northern Turf History*, 1949–50

Fairfax-Blakeborough, John, *A Short History of Redcar Racecourse*, 1951

Fisher, George, *Guinness Book of Turf Records*, 1964

Fitzgeorge-Parker, Tim, *The Spoilsports*, 1968

Fitzgeorge-Parker, Tim, *Ever Loyal: The Biography of Captain Neville Crump*, 1987

Francis, Dick, *The Sport of Queens*, revised edition, 1982

Francis, Dick, *Lester*, 1986

Fulford, Roger, *Votes for Women*, 1976

Galtrey, Sidney, *Memoirs of a Racing Journalist*, 1934

Good, Meyrick, *Good Days*, 1941

Good, Meyrick, *The Lure of the Turf*, 1957

Green, Reg, *A Race Apart*, 1988

Lambton, George, *Men and Horses I Have Known*, 1924

Loder, Eileen, *Bibliography of the History and Organisation of Horse Racing and Thoroughbred Breeding in Great Britain and Ireland*, 1978

Lucas, Pat, *Fifty Years of Racing at Chepstow*, 1976

Macey, Alan, *The Romance of the Derby Stakes*, 1976

Moorhouse, Edward, *The Romance of the Derby*, 1908

Mortimer, Roger, R. Onslow and P. Willett, *Biographical Encyclopaedia of British Flat Racing*, 1978

Morton, Charles, *My Sixty Years of the Turf*, 1930

Nightingale, Arthur, *My Racing Adventures*, 1907

Onslow, Richard, *Headquarters*, 1983

Payne, Ken, *The Coup*, 1978

Pegg, Norman, *Focus on Racing*, 1963

Prior, C.M., *History of the Racing Calendar and Stud Book*, 1926

Radford, Brian, *Taken for a Ride: An Insight into Racing Frauds*, 1981

Randall, John and Tony Morris, *Horse Racing: The Records*, 1985

Reinhardt, Molly, *The July Handicap*, 1973

Rodrigo, Robert, *The Racing Game*, 1958

Russell, Campbell, *Triumphs and Tragedies of the Turf*, 1930

Russell, Campbell, *Miracles of the Turf*, 1930

Scott, Brough and Gerry Cranham, *The World of Flat Racing*, 1983

Scott, Brough, *On and Off the Rails*, 1984

Seth-Smith, Michael, *Knight of the Turf*, 1980

Stevens, John, *Knavesmire*, 1984

Swaffer, Percy, *Fleet Street Goes Racing*, 1939

Tanner, Michael, *The Champion Hurdle*, 1989

Tresilian, Liz, *Aldaniti*, 1984

Warren, Charles (editor), *Sixty Years on the Turf*, 1903

Welcome, John, *Infamous Occasions*, 1980

Welcome, John, *Great Racing Disasters*, 1985

Weston, Tommy, *My Racing Life*, 1952

OTHER TITLES IN

THE
STRANGEST®
SERIES

The *Strangest* series has been delighting and enthralling readers for decades with weird, exotic, spooky and baffling tales of the absurd, ridiculous and the bizarre. This range of fascinating books – from Football to London, Rugby to Law and many subjects in between – details the very curious history of each one's funniest, oddest and most compelling characters, locations and events.

9781910232910

9781910232866

9781910232934

9781910232972

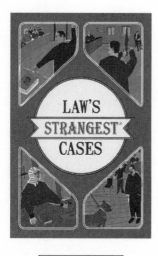

9781910232897

9781910232880

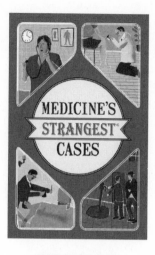

MEDICINE'S STRANGEST CASES

9781910232941

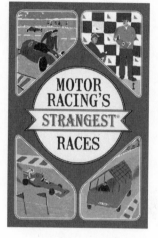

MOTOR RACING'S STRANGEST RACES

9781910232965

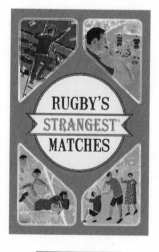

RUGBY'S STRANGEST MATCHES

9781910232873

RUNNING'S STRANGEST TALES

9781910232927

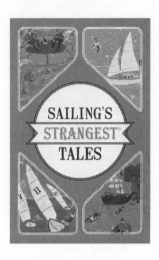

SAILING'S STRANGEST TALES

9781911042259

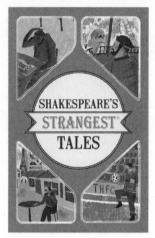

SHAKESPEARE'S STRANGEST TALES

9781910232903

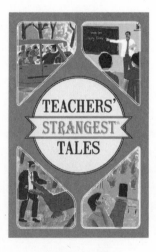

TEACHERS' STRANGEST TALES

9781910232989

TENNIS'S STRANGEST MATCHES

9781910232958